THE ECONOMICS OF DEVELOPMENT IN
SMALL COUNTRIES

Centre for Developing-Area Studies
McGill University
Keith Callard Lectures
Series I

THE ECONOMICS OF DEVELOPMENT
IN SMALL COUNTRIES WITH SPECIAL
REFERENCE TO THE CARIBBEAN

by
WILLIAM G. DEMAS

Montreal
PUBLISHED FOR THE CENTRE BY
MCGILL UNIVERSITY PRESS
1965

International Standard Book Number 07735-0044-8
Library of Congress Catalog Card No. 65-26563

The Centre for Developing-Area Studies, McGill
University, and the McGill University Press
gratefully acknowledge the support of the Canada Council,
whose grant in aid of publication made possible
the production of this volume.

TO
THE ECONOMISTS
OF THE
CARIBBEAN

FOREWORD

THE Centre for Developing-Area Studies was established at McGill University in the Fall of 1963. Designed on an interdisciplinary basis, the Centre aims to provide academic facilities for thoroughgoing study of the 'development' process in the economically less-advanced countries.

Three main types of activity are under way: building a core of knowledge and understanding of the developing areas; training students, both Western and non-Western, for university and public service at home and abroad; participating in technical-assistance programmes for sharing skilled human resources between advanced and developing countries. The Centre serves to co-ordinate and expand the relevant postgraduate studies in the social sciences at McGill. It is also expected that the University's course offerings at the undergraduate level will be enriched through the new programme. Initial emphasis is being placed on selected newly independent states of South Asia, West Africa, and the West Indies; this accords with the present distribution of expertise on the McGill faculty.

Professor Keith B. Callard was one of the major pioneers in this academic venture. The Centre's philosophy and structure —and, indeed, its very existence—are in a substantial degree the product of his vision, energy, and ability to articulate a worthwhile cause. His passing in 1961 deprived McGill and the academic community at large of the kind of scholarly resource which can never be replaced. At the early age of thirty-seven, Professor Callard had already made significant contributions to both teaching and research in the field of political science. And there was clear promise of bigger things to come. But this was not to be.

It seems altogether fitting to us, his colleagues, that his name be memorialized in a series of public lectures delivered at McGill by distinguished scholars, civil servants, and men of affairs concerned with accelerating the emergence from grinding poverty, ignorance, and disease of the vast underdeveloped part of the world. Professor Callard saw this as the great challenge of our era, and we are pleased to share it with him in this concrete way.

Mr. William G. Demas, Head of the Economic Planning Division of the Government of Trinidad and Tobago, served in 1964 as the first Research Fellow of the Centre. This book incorporates the four Callard Lectures delivered by him in March of that year. For our part, we shall be gratified if subsequent series match the quality of this effort.

IRVING BRECHER

Director
Centre for Developing-Area Studies

PREFACE

THIS book reproduces the substance of the four Keith Callard Lectures delivered by the author at McGill University in March 1964.

For about five months—from the end of January to the end of June 1964—it was my good fortune to be attached to the Centre for Developing-Area Studies at McGill University; and it was under the auspices of the Centre that I delivered the lectures.

While the substance of the lectures has been reproduced, they have been somewhat amplified in the course of rewriting —partly to incorporate the fruits of more mature reflection on the subject-matter and partly to take account of some of the helpful comments made by various people. But for the most part a 'spoken' rather than 'written' style has been retained in the interests of ease of presentation.

Most of the work so far done on problems of economic development has not sufficiently taken into account the size of countries. In the course of my work in the field of economic planning in Trinidad, I was led to question the relevance to small countries of much of the accepted doctrine on economic development. I came to the conclusion that a somewhat different approach was necessary for small countries, such as those in the Caribbean; and my views were fortified by the additional consideration that, partly because of their intermediate stage of economic development, the Caribbean countries had many unique features which distinguish them from many other small underdeveloped countries.

It is obvious that rational choices in the field of economic policy can be made only with the assistance of a relevant analytical framework. It is however often forgotten that, while economic analysis must have a place in this framework, there are other essential elements—geography; technology; and historical, social, political, and institutional factors.

The effort to provide such a framework to illuminate policy choices facing the Caribbean countries has to be made by the economists of the area, just as it has been made by the Latin American economists—especially those associated with the United Nations Economic Commission for Latin America. I therefore offer the following reflections on the political economy of small countries in general and of the Caribbean countries in particular so that the field can be explored more thoroughly (and no doubt more ably) by other economists in the Caribbean.

My only regret about the contents is that they do not incorporate more systematically organized empirical data. As I state in the first chapter, I have sought principally to put forward working hypotheses based on *a priori* analysis and observation of development patterns both historically and today in several countries, especially the Caribbean. The time available was much too short for me to undertake detailed statistical work covering the entire field with which I have dealt.

My debts are several.

First of all, a special word of thanks is due to Professor Irving Brecher, Director of the Centre for Developing-Area Studies, who invited me to McGill and asked me to deliver the Keith Callard Lectures, and to Professor James Mallory, Chairman of the Department of Economics and Political Science at McGill, who very kindly offered me the full facilities of the Department.

Second, there is the work of those writers to whose insights anyone working on development problems, however orthodox or heterodox he may be, must be indebted for many of his starting points—Arthur Lewis, Charles Kindleberger, and Albert Hirschman; Gunnar Myrdal, Hollis Chennery, and Dudley Seers. The last-named was good enough to read the manuscript and offer several constructive comments.

Next, there are those West Indian economists, discussions with whom over the last few years have done much to shape my ideas: Mr. Alister McIntyre and Mr. Lloyd Best of the University of the West Indies, and Mr. O'Neil Lewis and Mr. Frank Rampersad, my colleagues in the Government of Trinidad and Tobago. I received helpful comments on the manuscript from Mr. Rampersad. Not only did I receive helpful comments from Mr. McIntyre, I am also indebted to him for letting me read and quote in advance of publication his very incisive paper on *Decolonization and Trade Policy in the West Indies* (to be published by the University of Puerto Rico) and for a very instructive discussion on some of the problems of a highly open economy. I also benefited from an interesting discussion with Professor Charles Kennedy of the University of the West Indies.

Then there are those members of the staff of the McGill Department of Economics who also offered helpful comments: Professors Jack Weldon and Robert Mundell, and Mr. Antal Deutsch. Miss Adlith Brown, a West Indian graduate student at McGill, not only offered useful comments but kindly assisted with the compilation of data on the Caribbean.

My greatest debt is, however, due to Professor Kari Levitt of McGill with whom I had long discussions both before and after the delivery of the lectures and whose penetrating and constructive mind clarified much of my thinking.

Acknowledgements for permission to quote from F. Shebab, 'Kuwait: A Super-Affluent Society' are due to the editors of *Foreign Affairs*; from Bert Hoselitz, 'Patterns of Economic Growth' to the editors of the *Canadian Journal of Economics and Political Science*; from W. W. Rostow, *The Stages of Economic Growth* to the Cambridge University Press; and from W. A. Lewis, *Theory of Economic Growth* to Messrs. Allen and Unwin.

Finally, I must refer to the great assistance provided by Miss Teresa Seers, Librarian of the School of Commerce at McGill and her staff, by Mrs. Beatrice Hayes, Administrative Assistant of the Centre, and by Miss Beverley Carter, who had the arduous task of typing the manuscripts—which she performed cheerfully and diligently.

I should like to conclude this Preface with the usual reminder that the Trinidad and Tobago Government cannot be held responsible for the views expressed nor can those who offered comments be blamed for any of the errors and shortcomings.

WILLIAM G. DEMAS

Montreal and New York
June–July 1964

CONTENTS

TABLES

PART I: THE GENERAL FRAMEWORK

CHAPTER I: CRITERIA OF UNDERDEVELOPMENT, DEVELOPMENT, AND SELF-SUSTAINED GROWTH

My general theme is an exploration of the economics of development in small countries with particular reference to the Caribbean.

I shall take as my starting point an examination of the concepts of underdevelopment and self-sustained growth and the logical basis of the criteria often employed for empirical measurement of these phenomena. I shall argue that underdevelopment and self-sustained growth cannot be considered in isolation from the size of a particular country. I hope to be able to demonstate this proposition in the course of the first chapter as well as to throw some light on the meaning of the terms 'underdevelopment' and 'self-sustained growth'.

In the second chapter I shall deal more specifically with some of the difficulties faced by very small countries in achieving growth and breaking out of the vicious circle of underdevelopment in the contemporary world. There I shall outline alternative strategies of development open to these small countries.

In the third and fourth chapters, I shall relate some of these general considerations to the specific situation in the Caribbean and indicate special problems and opportunities facing economic planners and policy-makers in the Caribbean.

At the outset I wish to issue two important *caveats*. First, I should like to warn that the first two chapters will, to a large degree, take the form of working hypotheses. The subject is so relatively unexplored that it will be useful to start by putting forward general propositions based on *a priori* reasoning

3

and casual empiricism. For it is only with the aid of working hypotheses so derived that more rigorous empirical examination can proceed. Therefore, although I issue a *caveat*, I make no apology for the lack of systematic rigorous examination of data. However, the analysis and generalizations are based on more than casual examination of the contemporary situation in several economies and of the general lessons of economic history.

Second, I should like to make it clear that in discussing underdevelopment and self-sustained growth I shall not be dealing very extensively with the more fundamental social, political, and institutional parameters underlying the process of growth and structural change. I take this approach because I am not competent to do otherwise. I do, however, think there is merit in looking separately at the mechanics and configuration of economic development as reflected in the behaviour of economic variables. This might come as a disappointment to those who expect a more 'integrated' approach in a book on development written by someone attached to an institution which prides itself on an interdisciplinary approach to the development problem. But I am sure that there is something to be said for the view that the interdisciplinary approach is not inconsistent with a recognition of the virtues of the division of labour.

Ever since Rostow coined the term,[1] 'self-sustained growth' has been bandied about by laymen and economists alike.

The most common meaning given to the notion is a state of affairs in which a country can experience continued economic growth by relying on its own domestic savings to finance its domestic investment. This can alternatively be expressed in terms of balance being achieved in the international accounts of a country without resort to net capital imports. Increasingly, national development plans are doing precisely this, attempting to forecast the time when a country will be able to finance the capital formation necessary to achieve a desired rate of growth entirely from domestic savings.

This definition of self-sustained growth often leaves it unclear

[1] W. W. Rostow, 'The Take-off into Self-Sustained Growth', *Economic Journal*, March 1956.

4

whether only unrequited capital transfers or soft loans (i.e. aid) are being ruled out or whether the net inflow of private commercial capital is also to be excluded.

This definition also leaves unclear the type of economic structure likely to exist when the country has achieved what is claimed to be self-sustaining growth. In fact, however, any realistic assessment of the economic conditions likely to prevail in the country at the chosen future date would indicate vast problems of underdevelopment remaining to be solved, especially the problem of structural unemployment.[2] This lack of clarity again springs from concentrating on the domestic savings aspect. To judge from these exercises, one would think that the necessary and sufficient condition for the achievement of self-sustained growth is that the marginal savings ratio should exceed the average savings ratio for a period of about ten to twenty-nine years.

Again, in comparing the economic performance of different underdeveloped countries, it is often assumed that those countries with a relatively high *per capita* income are in some sense more 'developed' or nearer the takeoff point than other countries with a lower *per capita* income. Again, this tendency often springs from the use of a savings-centred model of development of the Harrod-Domar type, where global aggregates of savings, investment, and output are considered to be the central variables in the growth process.

There are also other ambiguities in the application of the concept. In addition, it is possible to detect all sorts of pleasing connotations of self-reliance and self-dependence which are at variance with the hard facts of international economic life in the contemporary world.

There are indeed several ambiguities and misconceptions in the concepts not only of self-sustained growth but also of underdevelopment and development; and these ambiguities stem from an incorrect appreciation of criteria of underdevelopment, development, and self-sustained growth.

[2] The projections of the time when self-sustained growth is likely to be achieved contained in India's Third Five-Year Plan and Nigeria's National Development Plan are cases in point.

To my mind, the two fundamental sources of ambiguity concerning self-sustained growth are to be found in the assumption that the level and rate of change of the *per capita* income of a country are uniquely related to its state of development and, second, the assumption—more often than not unconscious —that one is dealing with a closed economy which is also likely to be a very large one.

It is my view that the fundamental criterion of underdevelopment is the extent to which an economy has undergone structural transformation and has acquired the continuing capacity to adapt and to apply innovations. Furthermore, within the category of transformed economics, it is possible to have different degrees of 'self-sustenance' in the growth process, if I may coin a rather awkward word.

Let us consider the aspect of structural transformation first. We should begin by acknowledging that structural transformation is *usually* associated with a continuous increase in real income *per capita*. But the converse is not necessarily true. We must further acknowledge that transformation is also *usually* associated with an increase in the rate of domestic investment and the tendency to finance such investment largely from domestic sources; although, again, the converse is not necessarily true.

The misconceptions have arisen from regarding the development process purely as one of rising *per capita* income and increased domestic savings and investment.

I do not think it necessary to recapitulate Rostow's well-known stages of growth[3] nor to offer a critique of this schema, although I am well aware of the methodological objections to a 'stages' approach to human history. I am also aware of the statistical challenge which has been made to the notion of the takeoff period on the ground that there is no evidence that in the economic development of a large number of now advanced countries there was a sudden increase in either the investment ratio or the rate of growth of product.[4] I am here primarily

[3] W. W. Rostow, *The Stages of Economic Growth*, Cambridge, 1960.
[4] Cf. S. Kuznets, 'Notes on the Take-off' in Morgan, Betz, and Choudry, *Readings in Economic Development*, California, 1963.

concerned with *different kinds of growth* and am not concerned with whether or not, in fact, the notion of the takeoff is a historically valid one or what was or is the precise nature of the 'preconditions' for the takeoff.

Rostow himself distinguishes between four different types of contemporary underdeveloped countries:[5]

1. pre-takeoff economies where the savings and investment ratio—including limited net capital imports—is very low, less than 5 per cent of net national product;

2. economies attempting takeoff where the savings and investment ratios—including limited net capital imports—have risen above 5 per cent;

3. growing economies, where investment ratios—including limited net capital imports—have reached 10 per cent and over; and

4. enclave economies where (*a*) 'the apparent savings and investment rates, including substantial net capital imports, have reached 10 per cent or over but the domestic preconditions for sustained growth have not been achieved' or (*b*) 'net capital exports are large'.

It is with enclave economies of type 4 that I wish to deal. It is my contention that this conception of enclave economies is much wider than might at first sight be thought and that it throws much light on the real meaning of economic development.

This kind of economy may experience increases in certain important economic indices—such as the Gross Domestic Product, Domestic Capital Formation, Imports, and Exports—and the level of *per capita* national income may even attain 'respectably' high levels. This economic expansion may be due entirely to a boom in exports of the primary resource produced in the enclave sector of the economy, and the boom may be either short-lived or secular, depending on the physical availability of the particular commodity within the country at a reasonable real cost and on the price it commands in world markets. Where such secular economic expansion results in rising *per capita* income but the country remains an enclave

[5] Rostow, *Stages of Economic Growth*, pp. 43-5. All savings and investment rates are not of depreciation.

economy, it would be a profound mistake to infer that this growth in the enclave sector necessarily constitutes economic development or self-sustained growth.

For, quite apart from a sustained increase in *per capita* product and income, there are two essential characteristics of self-sustaining growth. The first aspect relates to saving and investment. Self-reinforcing growth normally requires the internal generation of sufficient domestic savings—in both the public and private sectors—to maintain the growth rate. This aspect is well recognized and has now been reduced to the status of a cliche.

The other aspect, although just as crucial, does not usually receive much attention. It may be termed the transformation of the structure of production.

I include seven basic elements in the term 'transformation of the structure of production'. These are the capacity to transform as determined by political and social processes and attitudes; the unification of the national market for goods and services; the shift of production and of labour as between primary, secondary, and tertiary sectors of the economy; the development of an increasing degree of interdependence among domestic industries and activities; changes in the importance and composition of foreign trade; the reduction of dualism in the economy; and the development of appropriate institutions.

First of all, transformation implies the development of the capacity of an economy to apply innovations continually and to adapt to changing situations, especially those originating abroad. Kindleberger attaches most importance to this last aspect; in fact, he calls it 'the capacity to transform',[6] and virtually identifies it with the ability to react to price and market situations. The capacity to transform is intimately tied up with those fundamental social and political processes and attitudes which, as I have stated, largely underlie the process of economic growth and structural change.

Second, it implies an increase in the transactions for markets

[6] See C. P. Kindleberger, *Economic Development*, New York, 1958, Chapter 7 and also his *Foreign Trade and the National Economy*, New Haven, 1962, Chapter 7.

as against subsistence production and the unification of fragmented localized markets into a national market, so that all the potential economies of scale within the national boundaries can be fully exploited.

Third, it implies a continuing process of reallocation of factors of production as between sectors of the national economy in accordance with changes in the relative productivity of different sectors and with changes in the composition of demand as *per capita* incomes rise. Statistically, this process manifests itself in the changing distribution of the labour force and the changing composition of output—from primary to secondary and tertiary activities.[7] There are also associated changes in the skill and occupational composition of the labour force, away from unskilled manual work to white-collar, service, professional, supervisory, and technical activities.

Fourth, it implies the forging of links between the various parts of the domestic production structure so that domestic industries become more 'interdependent' one with another. The interdependence manifests itself in the development of a whole network of forward and backward linkages[8] within the internal structure of production, whereby the products of an increasing number of industries become the inputs of other industries. This, in turn, implies a rapid growth of domestically produced 'intermediate' and capital goods.

[7] There is one important logical difficulty in using the share of tertiary production or services in either the composition of the Gross Domestic Product or in the distribution of the employed labour force. This is that a large share of services in an economy in terms of either product or employment may reflect either a high or low degree of structural transformation. On the one hand, a high proportion of labour employed in services may be simply a reflection of the existence of large numbers of disguised unemployed who flock into this sector for lack of productive or well-paid employment opportunities elsewhere. On the other hand, a high proportion in the tertiary sectors may be an index of a high degree of transformation in that it may reflect the changing composition of demand in favour of income-elastic products, such as entertainment or education, as *per capita* incomes grow.

[8] See A. Hirschman, *The Strategy of Economic Development*, New Haven, 1958, Chapter 6.

9

Fifth, as a consequence of the changing composition of demand away from goods towards services as dictated by relative income-elasticities of demand, of the creation of internal linkages in the economy, and of technological progress which not only economizes on the use of imported natural raw materials but also develops domestically produced synthetic materials, transformation tends to reduce the ratio of exports and imports to the Gross Domestic Product. But counterbalancing this tendency are three further forces. First, the effect of transformation in raising real income results in an increased demand for all goods, including imports. Second, to the extent that the early stages of transformation are accompanied by an increase in the rate of investment, there will be an increased demand for imported capital goods. Third, industrial development may give rise to increased imports of intermediate products, especially of raw materials.

The net effect of these opposing tendencies can be expressed in the following generalization. For all countries transformation is accompanied by an increase in the absolute volume of foreign trade and by a change in the composition of imports away from consumer goods and towards intermediate and capital goods. However, as we shall see, the ratio of foreign trade to Gross Domestic Product may fall *in the long run* for larger countries, but may remain stable, or even increase, for smaller countries. (Even in larger countries, the ratio may increase in the early stages of transformation as a result of sharp increases in imports of intermediate and capital goods.)

Next, transformation involves not necessarily an equalization but some reduction in the disparities between returns to factors of production within the national economy, these disparities constituting the phenomenon of 'dualism'.

One of the characteristics of underdevelopment is the dual economy, which may be defined as one in which different sectors of the national economy use techniques of widely different degrees of superiority and widely different factor proportions (especially capital relatively to labour), and where, in consequence, the marginal product of otherwise identical factors of production (and hence income earned) differs widely from sector to sector. It should be stressed that what is important here is productivity rather than income received; for, quite clearly, income received in a sector may differ from income produced because of subsidies received from other sectors or because of personal transfer payments to individuals within the sector, industry, or firm.

In this connection, it should be pointed out that the existence of a large volume of surplus labour, either completely unemployed or experiencing disguised unemployment, constitutes an extreme form of dualism; for the marginal product (and hence the income produced) of an unemployed worker is by definition zero, while that of an underemployed person is often in fact not greatly in excess of zero.

While the concept of economic dualism is clear enough, its application to economies in the real world is a somewhat elusive undertaking. To a significant extent, dualism in the sense in which it has here been defined is present in all economies—from the most advanced to the most underdeveloped—if only because of lack of complete factor mobility and of differences in production functions between sectors. There are significant gaps in output per man between the small and the large firm in the same industry in the U.S.A.[9] In the same country there are lagging regions and stubborn pockets of backwardness and underdevelopment. In the Soviet Union there is an enormous gap in output per man between heavy industry and agriculture. Therefore, the characterization of an economy as dual is in large part a matter of judgment. This difficulty can perhaps be clarified by developing the distinction between the existence of dualism as between economic sectors and between geographical regions of the country.

The question is whether or not the concept of transformation—and hence of self-sustained growth—ought to imply a fair

[9] Strictly speaking, dualism should only be discussed in terms of differences in the *marginal* product of a factor as between different uses. It is recognized that a large gap between output per man in different sectors is not necessarily an unambiguous index of dualism. But for statistical convenience we often have to use the *average* rather than the *marginal* product of labour.

degree of equality in *per capita* product and income between different *geographical regions* or between different *economic sectors* of the particular country. The two aspects have been lumped together by Myrdal who implies that both are necessary to the achievement of what he calls 'national economic integration'.[10]

It is my view that, although the distinction between the two aspects is a somewhat fine one, it is valid and operationally useful. I am inclined to think that in the initial stages of transformation of a national economy the second aspect of dualism —the increase in productivity per man and in the level of techniques employed in the backward sectors—is more important than the first aspect, the reduction of regional disparities. In other words, where the development process gets under way in one geographical region of a large country through, say, the expansion of exports of a leading sector, it might be more sensible to attempt to spread the effect of development throughout that region rather than attempt to pull up all regions at the same time. In this situation, or in a situation where there is no regional problem, dualism as between economic sectors of the region will be reduced by the diversification and expansion of the manufacturing sector and above all by the raising of productivity in the traditional agricultural sector, so that the complete dominance of the economy by the leading high-productivity sector is reduced by the expansion of and increase in productivity of other sectors. In the case of the 'enclave' economy this process depends upon the use of income generated in the dominant sector to provide investment funds and markets for the other sectors. But in other types of economy where the leading sector is not an 'enclave' industry it may also depend upon the extraction of savings from the traditional agricultural sector as it increases its productivity, as was done in Japan and the U.S.S.R.

It is important to note, however, that a high degree of transformation is compatible with a certain amount of continuing dualism between economic sectors. A good example is Japan in the nineteen-fifties. Principally because of the original density of population in relation to land at the time of Japan's takeoff

[10] Gunnar Myrdal, *An International Economy*, London, 1955, *passim.*

and the comparatively high rate of population growth, a feature of Japanese economic development has been the dual economy, with different factor proportions and hence differences in product per person employed between the technologically advanced large industrial units and the smaller labour-intensive units, often subcontracting for the larger units. It is one of the principal objectives of Japan's Long-Range Ten-Year Plan to eliminate the dual economy. But it should not be forgotten that agricultural productivity per acre and per man rose steadily in Japan from 1880 onwards. It remains true therefore that self-sustaining growth requires that the gap between the modern industrial sector and the agricultural sector be not too wide. The U.K. typifies the realization of this condition perhaps more than any other country in the world.

Disparities between different regions of the same national economy are another matter. It is obvious that in any dynamic economy certain regions must experience changing fortunes. There is the well-known decay of regions based on industries adversely affected by changes in technology and in external and internal demand conditions. Normally the sense of social cohesion in a developed national economy almost always leads to some kind of ameliorative action being taken, whether such action takes the form of retraining schemes, special inducements to capital to locate in the depressed areas, or transfer payments and subsidies. I am not referring to this kind of constantly shifting problem area. I am more concerned with chronically backward and geographically large areas which are chronically underdeveloped, such as the Brazilian North-East, the Italian South, or the Scottish Highlands in the U.K. The existence of such chronically backward areas for long periods is by no means inconsistent with self-sustained growth —unless, indeed, the backward or lagging region (or regions) is so large and so extremely backward as compared with the developed region or regions that geographical dualism comes to coincide with economic dualism. Thus the existence of South Italy can make of Italy a dual economy, whereas the existence of poverty in the Scottish Highlands does not make the U.K. a dual economy in the sense that Italy is one. It is my view

13

that, where the lagging region (or regions) is not too large and too backward relatively to the total size of the national economy, the problem of regional backwardness is usually tackled after the economy has reached a fairly advanced stage of transformation and proceeds more often than not from a social consciousness of the need for national equality in a geographical sense.

Be this as it may, it cannot be denied that national economic integration is essential to full economic transformation. For development of a national economy really means that all sectors—whether goods-producing or service-producing—and all regions become technologically progressive, *although not necessarily at the same rate.* For development means change and the incidence of change in the economic field is always uneven. But at the same time it remains true that development, if it means anything, means that production-functions are constantly changing and that capital is being constantly accumulated in all sectors and all regions. This is why an enclave economy— even one which yields a high level of *per capita* income and consumption to its inhabitants—cannot be considered truly developed.

Consider in this connection the Japanese economy. It has been undergoing structural transformation since the 1870's and has accumulated a large amount of capital from domestic savings. Yet in the late fifties the Japanese *per capita* income was still only $500 (U.S.) at official exchange rates. Japan has done much to realize its potential for development within the limits of prevailing technological knowledge, unlike many enclave economies. The reason for the relatively low level of Japan's *per capita* product and income is the ratio between its population and its stock of natural resources (including land and minerals) as compared to other better endowed enclave economies, which have however done less to realize their full potential. This merely illustrates the point that development involves a realization of productive potential in all branches and all regions of the national economy.

Dualism by economic sectors or by geographical regions can often correspond with social dualism, where people of identi-

14

fiable social or ethnic groups are concentrated in lagging sectors, backward regions, or low-paid occupations. In technical language, they constitute 'non-competing groups' since their opportunities for industrial, occupational, and sometimes even geographical mobility are restricted. Where such a state of affairs exists, the problem ceases to be an entirely economic one and assumes serious social dimensions. Social dualism is one of the features of a colonial economic structure,[11] but it is also to be found in societies which have long ceased to be colonial, such as Latin America. From a social point of view, an integrated national economy is one where all individuals, whatever their ethnic origin or social or economic background, have equal opportunity (legal, educational, and economic) to engage in any form of occupation or economic activity they may choose. Thus the social meaning of the elimination of dualism is equality of opportunity, which in turn is an important part of democracy. Just as very few countries can be said to be 'fully' democratic, so can very few, if any, countries be said to satisfy this ideal definition of social and economic integration, if only because different individuals start life with different economic (as opposed to legal and educational) opportunities. However, it is perhaps no accident that the most integrated national economies are also the most democratic societies (effectively and not just legally). Examples are the Scandinavian countries, Switzerland and, to a lesser extent, the United Kingdom.

Finally, underlying these economic manifestations of structural transformation and of a high savings and investment ratio, and indeed making them possible, is the development of a whole complex of supporting institutions—such as a capital market and other financial institutions, land tenure and agra-

[11] Figures of *per capita* national income for many African countries with an important mining enclave sector—such as the Congo (Leopoldville) and Northern Rhodesia (now called Zambia)—are quite meaningless because of the vast gap in *per capita* incomes between the Africans (the vast majority of the population) and the handful of Europeans. The gap between G.D.P. and national income is also quite large because of the remittance of profits to foreign shareholders. See the several studies of the U.N. Economic Commission for Africa.

rian systems, educational and training institutions, a developed system of public and business administration, and an appropriate structure of incentives, to mention only the more important ones.

Many economies have experienced growth of either short or long duration in the export sector. These are the celebrated export economies, producing mineral or raw material exports or tropical foodstuffs (produced either by peasants or by plantations) or temperate foodstuffs. The duration of such growth has depended on the secular demand conditions for their products in world markets and on the technological durability of their particular resources at not excessive real costs. But it is important to emphasize that in this kind of economy growth has been achieved often without a transformation of the production structure and has therefore been of a somewhat 'artificial' character. The important point is that in export economies under favourable conditions a high level of *per capita* income is possible without transformation. But when the particular dominant export encounters unfavourable conditions, its momentum of growth peters out. The maintenance on a permanent basis of a high level of income and rate of growth becomes possible only on the basis of a transformed economic structure. Some countries which started off as export economies have been able to achieve a high degree of transformation (New Zealand and Canada are good examples). But others have not.

To argue that *per capita* national income is not a satisfactory index of the degree of development is not to claim that international comparisons of national income are without meaning. This is an entirely different matter. I am well aware of the well-known difficulties of making international comparisons of standards of living and material welfare by using *per capita* national income figures. But I am of the view that comparisons of *per capita* national income are a rough guide to international differences in the level of material well-being attained, even after all allowances have been made for the conceptual and definitional difficulties, such as different income distributions, differences in the treatment of services as against production of physical commodities, differences in the relative coverage of

16

the money as against the subsistence economy, differences in the ratios between the prices of tradeable and non-tradeable goods in advanced as compared with less advanced countries, and so on and so forth.

In any event, even if one does not accept *per capita* national income figures as a guide to welfare, it is always possible to refine this measure by using more direct physical indices relating to the level of living, such as consumption of calories per person, number of doctors and teachers per person, literacy rates, weight of newsprint consumed per person, etc. But it will be found that these indices are fairly closely correlated with *per capita* real income.

My point is that, although comparisons of *per capita* income and *per capita* consumption of various physical quantities and services are a meaningful indicator of comparative levels of welfare, they do not tell us very much about the structure of the economy; they do not tell us whether or not the country is developed or underdeveloped, let alone whether or not growth is self-sustaining.

It follows from this definition of self-sustained growth that it is quite fallacious to equate the level or even rate of change of *per capita* national income with economic development. For an enclave economy can yield to its nationals high and rising levels of *per capita* income, consumption, and welfare without undergoing structural transformation, whereas an economy that has undergone a long period of transformation may still have a level of *per capita* income lower than that of an enclave economy.[12]

To see how an enclave economy can grow for a long time and yield increasing standards of living for the inhabitants, let us look at the following model, or rather caricature, of an imaginary enclave economy. Suppose a valuable mineral resource is discovered in a small hitherto predominantly agri-

---

[12] Compare the *per capita* income of Japan in 1960 of some $500 (U.S.) at official exchange rates with that of Kuwait, where the *per capita* oil revenues *alone* in 1963 amounted to $428 (U.S.). See Fakhri Shebab, 'Kuwait: A Super-Affluent Society', *Foreign Affairs*, April 1964, p. 463.

cultural island. Suppose further that the rate of growth of production and the price of the resource are such as to yield a rapidly growing Gross Domestic Product *per capita* in real terms. And suppose again that this state of affairs lasts for a long time —say forty years—and that the rest of the domestic economy remains unchanged. Then at the end of forty years both the level and rate of growth of real G.D.P. *per capita* in our mythical economy will be high. But quite clearly the economy will not be a developed one—even though it may come to have a higher *per capita* real product than a highly industrialized country.

If the national income (i.e. the income accruing to the residents of the country) grew at the same rate as the G.D.P. through a combination of fiscal measures and trade-union activity which had the effect of retaining a greater share of the profits for local use, there would certainly be an increase in *welfare*; but there would not be *development* in any meaningful sense of the term.

If, further, through the fiscal machinery the national income were very equitably distributed through, say, transfer incomes, this situation would be even better for *welfare*, but it would still not constitute *development*.

If, on the other hand, tax revenues were invested in social and economic overheads and in agricultural and industrial development, then the gap in productivity between the advanced mineral-exporting sector and the backward agricultural sector would be reduced and a diversified industrial sector might be developed; and this might set the stage for a real transformation of the structure of the economy. As agricultural productivity rose, there would be an increase in local purchasing power which would help industrial development and more 'residentiary' or market-oriented industries would be set up. As *per capita* income rose, there would be a shift of resources from agriculture to manufacturing and services as the composition of demand changed in accordance with Engel's Law. And as manufacturing grew, there would be more interindustry transactions arising, say, from the local processing of agricultural products and from the setting up of a local buildings-material

18

industry. This process would not only diversify the domestic production structure and make real product and income grow faster than they would otherwise do, but it would ultimately make the economy less vulnerable to an adverse change arising either from diminishing returns in the production of the mineral in the particular country or an unfavourable movement in the world terms of trade of the mineral *vis-à-vis* imported goods.[13] The capacity of the economy to continue growing with the complete disappearance of the mineral-resource sector would depend very much on whether or not it was a small or large country, as we shall see in the next chapter. In the course of this process the economy becomes more flexible and adaptable and is better fitted to cope with changing economic circumstances.

The point about this rather far-fetched parable was merely to stress the important fact that *per capita* G.D.P., or even national income, is not really a good index of the stage of development of a country which exports the product of a resource industry developed by foreign capital.

The real point is that development really means a structural transformation of the economy so that:

1. the degree of dualism between the productivity of different sectors, and at a later stage, different regions, is reduced;

2. surplus labour is eliminated and drawn into high-productivity employment;

3. subsistence production is eliminated and a national market is established for goods and services;

4. the share of manufacturing and services in Gross Domestic Product is increased in response to the changing composition of demand;

[13] With regard to Kuwait, F. Shebab has written: 'One basic question has always been asked: how long is it going to last? The Kuwaitis are quite alive to the precariousness of their riches. Anxiety over the future dominates their thoughts and many of their actions. It is evident in the attempt to build up their social capital, to set up an organized public service and to foster rapid industrial development; it is evident in the determined effort to accumulate foreign reserves; and above all, it is evident in the desire to achieve all this in a desperately short time. Haste is, indeed, the order of the day.' Shebab, p. 464.

5. the volume of interindustry transactions increases, mainly as a result of the growth of the manufacturing sector;

6. the ratio of imports to G.D.P. falls *in the long run*—although the volume of imports increases absolutely—and the composition of imports shifts away from consumer to intermediate and capital goods; and

7. the economy becomes not only more diversified but more flexible and adaptable, as a result of underlying political, social, and institutional changes.

Structural transformation is therefore an indispensable element in self-sustained growth. If it were possible to devise a single index to measure the development of an economy it would have to be one which takes the above factors into account either together with or instead of the *per capita* G.D.P.[14]

An economy that has undergone structural transformation is one that is able to continue adapting itself to changed circumstances and to changing production functions by introducing innovations. This does not mean, as we shall see, that it is necessarily in the vanguard of introducing innovations. It can be merely imitative in technology. And, as we shall see presently, the smaller national economies are, the more adaptable and flexible their structures must be if they are to attain sufficient independence from changing external conditions.

We have therefore seen that structural transformation is the real criterion of underdevelopment and self-sustained growth. But I now come to my second point. There are different degrees of 'self-sustenance' in growth patterns. It is quite possible for an economy to have achieved structural transformation and yet not be *fully* self-sustaining. It is my contention that fully self-sustaining growth is possible only in a very large—in terms of both area and population—continental type economy.

Most growth theorists and even development economists—if I may be allowed to make the distinction—usually assume large closed economies. While this is often to be excused as a heuristic devise, it can be most misleading when the conclusions drawn from such closed models are carelessly brought

[14] As we have seen, care must however be exercised in using employment or product originating in the tertiary sector.

to bear on the development process in a very large number of countries.

These strictures apply not only to the formal post-Keynesian growth models of Harrod-Domar parentage which have proliferated in recent years. They apply with no less force to policy models which claim to prescribe the path which under-developed countries should consciously seek to follow in order to achieve planned or semi-planned development. The 'Soviet' model of development and some of the versions of the balanced growth doctrine are cases in point. We shall discuss the limitations of the Soviet model, the post-Keynesian growth models, and some versions of the balanced growth model in the second chapter. Even Rostow who, as an historian is very much aware of the historical role of foreign trade in the process of economic growth, does not always seem to realize the full implications of a highly open economy for the pattern and character of growth. His very concept of self-sustained growth, suggesting as it does a closed-circuit' flow, implies a large autonomous self-sufficient economy with a rounded structure of production, including a capital-goods sector, and with its momentum of growth determined by internal factors and not by external factors, such as foreign trade and capital inflows.[15]

The fact is that many, if not most, national economies are not autonomous in that they do not have a domestic capital-goods sector and are open in varying degrees in the sense of either trade or capital imports. What is more, both the absence of a capital-goods sector and the degree of openness are, to a large extent, structurally determined by the size of the economy. Once we realize this, we have to modify the notion of self-sustained growth to allow for varying degrees of dependence in the pattern of growth.

I now turn to the definition of size. I have intentionally left size to this stage of the argument for it is my view that the question of size is very relevant to the *character* of, if not to the *possibility of achieving*, structural transformation. In the next chapter I shall analyse specifically the advantages and dis-

[15] As the subsequent argument makes clear, this is more than a semantic point.

advantages of size for the development of those underdeveloped countries which are small.

By size I mean nothing more than the *absolute number of persons living in a national economy and its land area.* I deliberately exclude either *per capita* income or the aggregate purchasing power of the country as measured by the product of numbers of persons and *per capita* income. The question of land area however raises difficult problems. The sort of country which I have mainly in mind is one that is small in both absolute population and land area. Some are of the view that a small country is one that has less than 10 million inhabitants.[16] Coming from a very small island, I am inclined to the view that a small country is one with less than 5 million people and 10,000 to 20,000 square miles of usable land. But the argument of this chapter is not greatly affected whether we use an upper limit of 5 or 10 million inhabitants. I consider a very large country as one with a population of more than 100 million and with more than 1 million square miles of territory. In this connection countries like Canada and Australia raise very awkward problems. For one thing, they have more inhabitants than our upper limits, 18 million and 10·5 million respectively in 1961. For another, their areas are among the biggest land masses in the world. But it can be argued that both Canada and Australia have large amounts of unusable land area, given the present 'state of the arts'.

It is quite obvious that the size of a country in this sense imposes certain constraints on the pattern of growth and hence on the character and degree to which such growth can be self-sustaining.

The pattern of growth in a very small country must of necessity be different from that in a large continental country. This is so for two fundamental reasons. First, resources in a small country are likely to be highly skewed, while the composition of domestic demand for goods and services will be more diversified. Hence most small countries must of necessity

[16] S. Kuznets, 'Economic Growth of Small Nations', *Economic Consequences of the Size of Nations*, ed. by E. A. G. Robinson, London, 1960, p. 14.

exchange the products of their few specialized resources against a great variety of imported goods. Second, economies of scale reinforce this first tendency and make it necessary to produce for a market wider than the domestic market. Hence most small countries have both a high ratio of exports to G.D.P. as well as a concentrated composition of exports and a diversified structure of imports. Such countries trade more and are also more specialized than large ones.[17]

What might appear to be an exception to this generalization can easily be explained. There is some evidence that a colonial economic structure makes for a high dependence on foreign trade, irrespective of the size of the country.[18] Colonial economic policy tends to encourage countries to export primary products and to neglect positive measures for import-substitution, even where the country may have the variety of resources and the domestic market. So long as colonial economic policies are enforced, the country remains an export economy. But, with transformation, the foreign trade ratio will certainly fall in the long run.

Economists associated with the 'structuralist' school of thought largely developed by Prebisch and others at E.C.L.A. have paid much attention to the interaction between foreign trade and the process of economic growth. They are concerned not merely with the distribution of the gains from trade be-

[17] See the data in Kindleberger, *Foreign Trade*, pp. 34–5. Also Kuznets, 'Economic Growth', pp. 18–23. The two factors—size of population and land areas—are both important. Even though 'intermediate' cases such as Australia and Canada have large land areas (even after allowing for what is unusable) and consequently a wide variety of resources, their relatively small population tends to make for a relatively small home market. Hence foreign trade is of great importance to such countries. See also Deutsch, Bliss, and Eckstein, 'Population, Sovereignty, and the share of Foreign Trade', *Economic Development and Cultural Change*, July 1962, pp. 353–66.

[18] See Deutsch and others, 'Population, Sovereignty etc'. The Congo (Leopoldville) is a good case in point. Although it has large and varied natural resources and a population of some 14 million, its ratio of exports to G.D.P. in 1960 was as high as 42 per cent. (Calculated from U.N. Economic Commission for Africa, *Industrial Growth in Africa*, New York, 1963, p. 2, Table I.)

tween developed and underdeveloped countries, as is commonly believed, but also with such questions as the interrelationships between the rate of growth of a country's external trade and the rate of growth of its total production, between the rate of growth of its exports and its imports, and between its structure of exports and imports and the composition of domestic production. This approach has made an important contribution to an understanding of the process of growth. As an explanation of inflation, structuralism is by no means complete,[19] but it yields important insights into the relationship between the foreign trade sector and the internal economy, into problems of economic policy and of planning, and into the problems of economic integration among underdeveloped countries.[20]

In fact Dudley Seers has recently thrown much light on the problem of the stages of growth in primary-producing countries in the twentieth century by applying structuralist ideas.[21] He has developed a 'stages' approach to industrialization in such countries in terms of a movement from exporting primary products with very little manufacturing to producing manufactured consumer goods in replacement of imports, then to import-substitution in intermediate and capital goods. The last

[19] The most rigorous exposition of the structuralist theory of inflation is Dudley Seers, 'A Theory of Inflation and Growth', *Oxford Economic Papers*, June 1962. For a critique of the structuralist position on inflation, see W. A. Lewis, 'Observations on the Relationship between Inflation and Economic Development', *Proceedings of Conference on Inflation and Economic Development*, Rio de Janeiro, January 1963. The structuralist theory has never been able to answer satisfactorily the question why in countries suffering from the same 'structural' factors as the Latin American countries—e.g. India—inflation has not spiralled.

[20] For an excellent analysis of the interaction between the foreign trade sector and the internal economy, see the E.C.L.A. Document presented to the U.N. Conference on Trade and Development, *Latin America and the U.N. Conference on Trade and Development*, February 1964, E/Conf. 46/71.

[21] Dudley Seers, 'The Stages of Economic Development of a Primary-Producer in the Twentieth Century', *The Economic Bulletin of Ghana*, VII, No. 4, 1963, 57–69.

two stages are, first, exporting manufactures to partner countries in an integrated area and, second, exporting such goods to world markets. Each stage is accompanied by appropriate institutional changes in the form of tariffs, import controls, foreign exchange controls, monetary arrangements, policies towards foreign capital, etc. And changes in policies and institutions are found to stem from political decisions triggered off by pressures from the population for higher standards of living and more employment and by the changes in power and influence of various social and economic groups.

Whatever one may think of this particular 'stages' approach, the fact remains that, as a result of the work of the structuralists, no one can now study an underdeveloped economy without looking very closely indeed at the size and composition of its foreign trade in relation to the volume and structure of its domestic production and at the type of monetary, commercial, and foreign exchange policies which it pursues.

Certain conclusions about the growth pattern of small countries can be drawn.

First, the degree of structural interdependence between the various sectors of the domestic economy is less for small countries with a highly skewed distribution of natural resources than for larger countries with a more balanced distribution of resources. While, generally speaking, an increasing degree of interdependence in the structure of domestic production is an index of economic transformation, we must expect the process to stop sooner in a small than in a large country. One of the most important areas for economic research is, I believe, the international comparison of interindustry relationships in the light of differences in aggregate population and *per capita* income.[22]

Second, and as a corollary of the first point, since most interdependence occurs in and through the development of the manufacturing sector,[23] for any given ratio of manufacturing

[22] Cf. W. Leontief, 'The Structure of Development', *Technology and Economic Development*, New York, 1963, pp. 105–24.

[23] Cf. H. B. Chenery and T. Watanabe, 'International Comparisons of the Structure of Production', *Econometrics*, October 1958, pp. 493–4.

production to G.D.P. a small country will rely more heavily on foreign imports than a large country.

Thirdly, when there are no exportable products of resource industries, we should expect manufactured goods to loom larger in total exports, the smaller the size of the country. Switzerland and Belgium are good examples.[24]

These facts also have important corollaries for statistical work on comparisons of economic growth and structure. If we are seeking to measure statistically the degree of transformation of different national economies, even those with the same level of *per capita* income, we should expect that smaller countries would show less industrial interdependence, more trade relatively to total production, a more specialized composition of exports, and a more specialized labour force than larger countries. In other words, in such comparisons we have to bear in mind the degree of dependence on foreign trade.

Now if we apply our criterion of structural transformation alone, we may hazard the judgment that in this sense the economies of Australia, New Zealand, Denmark, Japan, and Canada are self-sustaining while those of the Caribbean, Latin American, and Middle East oil-producing countries are not. For all the economies in the first category have undergone structural transformation in the sense defined above, in spite of the fact that Canada, Australia, New Zealand, and Denmark are principally exporters of primary products and that Japan has a lower *per capita* national income than either Venezuela or Kuwait, although its economy has been undergoing a continuous process of structural transformation since the 1870's. With regard to Canada, Australia, New Zealand, and Denmark, it is worth pointing out that the share of manufacturing in both output and employment greatly exceeds the share of agriculture and mining.

However, Canada, Australia, and New Zealand are all net importers of long-term capital. And this on the face of it appears to be inconsistent with the usual definition of self-

---

[24] See the Chapters on Switzerland and Belgium in Robinson, ed., *Economic Consequences of the Size of Nations.*

sustained growth in terms of the sufficiency of domestic savings to finance domestic investment.

The first thing to be said about capital inflow is that the smaller the country, the greater the probability that foreign capital inflow can contribute a significant portion of total domestic capital formation. A large country, simply because it is large, will make huge drafts on foreign savings if it is to be highly dependent on such savings.[25] A small country can therefore become a highly dependent economy in respect of both trade and capital flows.

At this stage it is worth while exploring the relationship between aid, private capital inflows, and the degree of development of a country. We have to distinguish between aid (soft loans and grants) and international movements of private capital in search of profit. One of the confusing things about the use of the term 'aid' in recent years has been the inclusion of these two quite separate things under one label. While all net capital inflows add to the real resources available to a country, it is very useful to reserve the term 'aid' for the inflow of foreign funds which are not motivated by the ordinary commercial criteria.

An economy that has achieved an advanced degree of transformation does not usually require aid—in the sense specified above—but it may still import fairly large amounts of private commercial capital.[26] But it does not follow that all underdeveloped economies which have not achieved much transformation require large amounts of economic aid. This is especially true of prosperous enclave economies where there is not much population pressure or structural unemployment. Kuwait seems to be a very good case in point. This country

[25] Cf. Kuznets, 'Economic Growth', p. 23.

[26] Rosenstein-Rodan distinguishes between sustained growth and self-sustaining growth. In the former situation, the economy develops the ability to absorb technical progress and begins to develop a differentiated production structure—the early stages of what I here call 'transformation'. In the second stage, transformation goes further and the economy no longer requires external aid. See P. N. Rosenstein-Rodan, 'International Aid for Underdeveloped Countries', *Review of Economics and Statistics*, May 1961, p. 113.

receives so much revenue from oil that not only can it satisfy its own needs for social overhead capital but it can also lend vast amounts of money to other Arab countries through the Arab Development Fund.[27] On the other hand, there may be several less prosperous enclave economies suffering from severe problems of overpopulation, unemployment, and underemployment which may find the revenues yielded by their enclave sectors insufficient to provide them with the wherewithal to transform their economic structures. This may be so, even if these countries have a *per capita* income higher than the majority of other underdeveloped countries. In short, the economic criteria now explicitly or implicitly employed for the receipt of aid and special trade treatment are somewhat inadequate. The *per capita* national income of a country is the most commonly used yardstick; but this is inadequate. If it is the purpose of economic aid and special trade treatment to help countries transform their economic structures and achieve whatever degree of self-sustained growth is possible—given their size and degree of openness—more complex criteria will have to be used in making a judgment of the amount of aid required or whether the country should get special trade treatment. This is not the place to develop such criteria. But it is suggested that, besides the usual *per capita* income figure, other factors such as the outlook for the principal export commodity or commodities, the degree of the economy's dependence on such commodity or commodities, the amount of structural unemployment and underemployment, the extent of overpopulation, the extent of dualism in the economy, and the state of development of its capital market should be considered.

As we have just seen, both aid and commercial capital inflow add to the real resources of the recipient country in that it is thereby enabled to absorb for investment or consumption purposes more resources than it currently produces. This means, other things being equal, that the receipts of either aid or net capital inflow will reduce the volume of domestic savings required to maintain a given rate of economic growth. But, given the policy of the recipient country, the volume of private capital

[27] Shehab, 'Kuwait', p. 474.

inflow into industries other than resource industries tends to be correlated with its state of development. It is quite possible that Australia and Canada, which are well-known net importers of private commercial capital in the manufacturing sectors of their economies, could make tolerable advances in *per capita* product and income without drawing on foreign savings, although this would certainly entail some degree of sacrifice. On the other hand, a country like India would certainly find its efforts at transformation critically handicapped without the inflow of foreign resources in the form of aid. But once transformation is under way and the economy keeps growing, it is quite possible that, depending on the policy of the government towards private foreign investment, the volume of inflow of foreign resources in the form of commercial capital could greatly exceed the volume it received previously in the form of foreign aid.

Given its policy, the volume of private capital inflow into a country depends upon three other things: (*a*) its development and prospects for further growth, (*b*) the state of its capital market, and (*c*) whether it is a large producer and exporter of resource products.

Here the policy of the country towards foreign private capital is the basic parameter. This is quite obvious and needs no further elaboration. Today many underdeveloped countries—whether for good or bad reasons—are somewhat suspicious of private foreign investment and, where such inflow is permitted, it is often hedged around with several restrictions and conditions designed to safeguard what is conceived to be the national interest. Often, too, entire sectors of the economy are excluded from such investment. Some countries, like India, reserve certain sectors of the economy for public operations only, while in others, like Norway, foreign capital is not allowed in for the development of natural resources on the grounds that such resources should be owned only by nationals.

Second, given the policy in force, recourse to the import of private long-term capital, both by the public and private sectors, becomes necessary because of the underdeveloped state of the domestic capital market, especially for long-term paper. In

29

this connection it should be pointed out that there are really very few countries with fully developed capital markets[28] and that underdeveloped capital markets are not peculiar to underdeveloped countries. Recently, several developed European countries have been borrowing long from the New York capital market and at the same time have been piling up foreign exchange reserves. This *prima facie* indicates that there was no real shortage of domestic savings; rather it suggests that the domestic capital markets were unable to bring savers and borrowers together on terms considered mutually advantageous. Even a highly developed country with a transformed economic structure may therefore for this reason borrow long-term capital from abroad for either business or governmental use.

Third, and given again the policy of the recipient country, we find that, broadly speaking, the more developed a country is and the better its economic prospects, the more it is likely to receive foreign capital inflow. Such investment often takes the form of tariff factories assisting in the process of import-substitution, as in Canada and Australia. This is merely another illustration of the well-known principle 'unto everyone that hath shall be given'. It has often been observed that rates of return in manufacturing industry tend to be higher in the developed as compared with the less developed countries and that the bulk of the U.S. foreign investment since the war in manufacturing industry has been in the developed countries of Western Europe, Australia, and Canada. Here we must distinguish sharply between the primary-producing sector and the other sectors of the economy, especially manufacturing. For, as we shall see in a moment, foreign investment in resource industries or primary-producing enclaves has nothing to do with the level of development of the economy.

Consideration of the resource aspect raises several important and interesting issues. First of all, it raises the question whether the unit of study in the field of economic development ought to

[28] Compare C. P. Kindleberger, 'European Economic Integration and the Development of a Single Financial Centre for Long-Term Capital', *Veltwirtschaftliches Archiv*, XC, No. 2, 1964, 189–210.

be the national economy, the regional economy,[29] the trading bloc, the world economy, or indeed the international corporation.

I am unequivocally of the opinion that the nation is a valid concept in economic analysis, even though I hope to demonstrate in the next chapter the several problems faced in the contemporary world by small nations with heavy population densities. But we must admit that in order to understand many of the phenomena of the world economy over the last two hundred years we have to concede that there are units of economic activity which either transcend or ignore national boundaries. In this connection, we have to recall the 'pôles de croissance' or 'poles of development' of Professor Perroux[30] and the other French students of the growth and structure of economies. These poles of development have 'effets d'entraînement' both within national economies and beyond the boundaries of nations. One can think in this context of either large international corporations producing natural resources in as many countries as they can be found, or of large industrial complexes such as the Ruhr which demand inputs from and supply outputs to industries in several nations, even without economic integration in the form of customs unions or free trade areas. Or one can think of the British economy of the nineteenth century which in a very real sense was an Atlantic economy, as a consequence of which investments were made in North American railways in order to provide food for the workers who manned the factories of the 'workshop of the world'. Or one can call to mind John Stuart Mill's famous dictum that in the nineteenth century the sugar colonies of the West Indies were not really economies separate from Britain in any meaningful sense but merely 'the place where England finds it convenient to carry on the production of sugar, coffee, and a few other tropical commodities. . . . The trade of the West Indies is therefore hardly to be considered as external trade,

[29] The term 'regional' is used here and in the rest of the chapter to mean a group of neighbouring countries.

[30] See François Perroux, *L'Economie du XXᵉ Siècle*, Paris, 1961.

but more resembles the traffic between town and country.'[31]

In short the national economy can be a very dependent one in the sense that decisions taken by large international corporations or by other countries can profoundly affect not only the momentum but the entire pattern of growth. In the extreme case it may even become a satellite economy. What is the real meaning of self-sustained growth in a satellite economy?[32] I must confess that I do not know.

This brings us to a very important point indeed. Self-sustained growth in the sense which includes not only structural transformation but dependence on domestic savings and on domestically generated poles of growth is more likely to be achieved in a large self-contained continental economy such as the U.S.A. and the U.S.S.R. and potentially perhaps in India and China than in small countries. A continental economy usually has access to a very wide range of resources simply

[31] J. S. Mill, *Principles of Political Economy*, London, 1892, pp. 454-5. The *Principles* were first published in 1848.

[32] The term was coined by Bert Hoselitz. See his 'Patterns of Economic Growth', *Canadian Journal of Economics and Political Science*, XXI, 1955, 420-1. In this article, the writer makes a distinction between 'dominant' and 'satellitic' patterns of economic growth. 'The ideal case', he continues, 'of a dominant pattern would be exhibited by a country with a fully closed economy, with no need to resort to foreign borrowing for purposes of capital accumulation, and without exports. At the other extreme we would have a society which draws all its capital for development from abroad and which develops only those branches of production whose output is entirely exported. If we further stipulate that all or the bulk of capital imports come from one source and that all or the bulk of the exports go to one destination, we have the ideal typical case of a country with a satellitic pattern of growth.' The writer goes on to state that the Swiss and Danish economies have exhibited satellitic patterns of growth. I would not stretch the word 'satellitic' to include the Swiss and Danish patterns of development. I would rather consider them as a case of highly open economies with 'the capacity . . . to adjust their productive pattern to the needs and opportunities of the countries surrounding them'. I think the crucial distinction ought to turn on who makes the vital economic decisions and this depends not only on dependence of the economy on exports to two or three principal trading partners but on the extent of foreign ownership of the capital stock of the country.

32

because it covers such a large area and can consequently be self-sufficient in respect not only of trade but also of 'pôles de croissance'. Its momentum of growth can be fully self-determined and internal. Thus it does not need to rely on foreign demand to give both short-run and long-run momentum to its economy. The share of foreign investment in total capital formation may also not be as large as in a smaller country where a mineral or raw material-producing sector financed by foreign capital may dominate the whole economy. And the decisions of its producers and its government are relatively independent of the decisions of producers and governments in other countries. A very large continental country may also be able to escape dependence on one or two large principal customers and the geographical distribution of its export trade may be highly diversified.[33] This means that in the continental economy structural transformation can get under way and can continue without critical reliance on foreign trade, on foreign capital, or on foreign decisions. (This statement of course omits the problems raised by the necessity to 'finance' the takeoff even in such very large economies. We shall return to this theme in our next chapter.)[34]

We therefore have to come to the conclusion that the fullest degree of 'self-sustenance' in the growth process is possible only in a very large continental-type economy.

This raises another important aspect of self-sustained growth,

[33] Cf. A. Hirschman, *National Power and the Structure of Foreign Trade*, Berkeley, 1945; Kindleberger, *Foreign Trade and the National Economy*, pp. 143–7; and Kuznets, 'Economic Growth', p. 23.

[34] It should however be noted that large (e.g. the U.S.A.) or medium-sized (e.g. the U.K.) developed economies which are open on the side of capital movements can have their momentum of internal development conditioned by the factor of openness. In large part the openness in respect of capital movements in these two economies derives from two facts. First, since they have highly developed capital markets, many other countries wish to borrow from them. Second, their currencies are used as international reserve currencies. Institutional reform of the international monetary system aiming at providing more international liquidity can easily remove the effects of such openness in restricting growth in these two economies.

the question of innovational dynamism. While a change in production functions is essential for the takeoff both in respect of the manufacturing and the agricultural sectors, if only to eliminate 'dualism', and continuing changes are necessary in any structurally transformed economy which is progressing, there is an essential difference between economies which are active centres of innovation and economic organization and those which are innovationally inert or passive, even where both sets of countries are heavily dependent on foreign trade. The former are usually the countries where innovations are first to take place and the first to be applied. These are the countries with a predominance of 'poles of growth'. They include most of the metropolitan countries. By their very nature countries dominated by resource exports are not technological leaders in this sense. But an economy such as Japan which has to fight to preserve and improve its place in international competition in manufactures has of necessity become very innovationally dynamic. This distinction cuts across that between large and small economies. In fact, while most large transformed economies which follow a closed pattern of development are likely to be innovationally dynamic, smaller open economies may be either dynamic or inert in this respect. The distinction turns largely on whether the open economy is an exporter of resource products or manufactured goods and on the extent to which the assets belong to and are therefore subject to the decisions of nationals or foreigners.[35]

Let me clear up some possible misconceptions as to what I have said about resource industries. First, and obviously, there is nothing good or bad in relying on exports of resource products and on the foreign capital usually associated with their development. There is always, of course, the possibility of depletion of domestic supply or an extinction of foreign demand. This is why it makes sense to develop manufacturing industries based on the domestic market and, if possible, export markets as well. Such development usually tends to occur on the basis

[35] The connection between a high degree of self-sustenance in the growth pattern and innovational dynamism has been pointed out to me by Professor Kari Levitt of McGill University.

of a rise in demand for the products of 'residentiary' or location-based manufacturing industries as a result of a change in the composition of demand as *per capita* income increase; and this process is often assisted by tariffs. The dependence on foreign capital and resource industries is basically a policy decision. A negative decision has consequences for the pattern of development, although it will usually make *per capita* incomes lower than they would otherwise be, at least for a very long time indeed. In any event it would be foolish for a small country with heavy population pressure not to encourage resource development by foreign capital, provided of course satisfactory fiscal and other arrangements can be secured. In any event the fiscal revenues derived from such industries can and should be used to help transform the economic structure through overhead and directly productive investments, vocational training, and education. A small and overpopulated country is usually very lucky if it has resource industries.

Before I end I must draw attention to one of the most important implications of my remarks on self-sustaining growth and small countries. I have already raised the question as to what unit of economic activity should be considered in relation to the problem of self-sustained growth. I also stated that I believed the nation to be a valid concept in economic analysis. But at the same time it is impossible to ignore the fact that in many important economic respects the political boundaries which define a nation geographically are rather artificial. It follows from this that, other things being equal, the larger the geographical size and population of the unit involved, the more nearly can the growth process approximate the continental pattern and the more nearly can the pattern of growth become fully self-sustaining. Quite clearly, the world as a whole is a closed economy. All of this sounds obvious enough, but the important implication is that economic regionalism offers one important avenue for many small underdeveloped countries to achieve the possibility of a more fully self-sustained pattern of growth.

Now, most nations by definition feel very strongly about the retention of sovereignty in as many fields as possible, and a federal solution may not always be acceptable. This therefore implies that, at least as a start, economic regionalism in some fields with decisions resting on mutual agreement will have to be combined with purely national decisions on economic policies in others. Economic regionalism in itself is not the complete answer, since many of the feasible economic regions may still be too small in terms of both area and population when compared with continental economies of the size of the U.S.A., India, China, the U.S.S.R., or, indeed, the European Economic Community, or the Latin American Free Trade Area; but at least some regional co-operation or some limited measure of economic integration may be better than none at all, and any move towards regionalism will be a step in the right direction.

As we shall see in the next chapter, the value of regional economic integration in terms of development patterns is that it makes possible a strategy of development based on import-substitution rather than export creation and therefore a less 'dependent' pattern of development. Some of the external transactions of the member-nations of the integrated area become 'internal' to the region. Moreover, in so far as there are economies of scale in capital markets, the pooling of national capital markets might lead to the generation of more domestically financed investment.

We can therefore conclude that, although the national economy is a valid concept from many points of view, the regional economy may in several important respects be just as significant in terms of the possibility of realizing a less dependent pattern of economic growth. But we shall have more to say on the economics of integration in the next chapter.

I should like to conclude by pointing out that my remarks about small transformed economies not being fully self-determining in an economic sense do not imply that the objective of becoming transformed or self-sustaining is to free oneself from the necessity of engaging in foreign trade or from importing commercial capital. Nor am I arguing in favour of the pursuit of autarchic policies. Either inference would be clearly absurd for several reasons. First, as we have seen, the absolute volume of imports of a country, if not the ratio of imports to G.D.P., rises with transformation. There is also a change in the composition of imports, especially in favour of intermediate and capital goods, but not an absolute decline in the total. Second, barring a drastic and wholly improbable change in the world's political arrangements, there will, for the foreseeable future, even with a widespread move towards regional economic integration, remain a large number of small countries which will be very dependent on trade and possibly also on private commercial capital inflows. Third, it is a well-known fact that the increase in international trade in recent years has been most rapid between highly developed, transformed economies. There are no antitrade or anti-international capital inflow implications in my analysis.

To put the thesis of this chapter into focus, I shall attempt to summarize the argument very baldly in the form of the following propositions:

1. The criterion of development or underdevelopment of a country is the extent to which it has achieved structural transformation. Indices of transformation would include shares of agriculture, manufacturing and services in the G.D.P. and in employment, the degree of structural interdependence in the economy, the difference in productivity per man between various sectors and regions within the economy, and the extent to which disguised and open unemployment have been eliminated.

2. Structural transformation is usually associated with an increase in real output and real income per head.

3. A country can have a high *per capita* income without having undergone structural transformation, if it is an enclave economy or a small economy relying on exports of valuable natural-resource products.

4. In this case continued increases in income per head over the indefinite future depends either on the resource lasting and commanding a good price in world markets or on the economy undergoing structural transformation.

5. A transformed economy is one that is flexible and adaptable and ready to apply technological and institutional innovations.

37

6. A very small country can achieve transformation only with a high ratio of foreign trade to G.D.P.

7. Only large continental economies with varied resources and very large populations can achieve fully self-sustaining growth.

8. Small countries, even if their economies have undergone transformation, are placed in various degrees of dependence in that their momentum of growth is not fully determined by decisions of domestic producers, consumers, and the local government.

9. To some extent even in transformed small economies the national economy may not in many important respects be the really important unit of economic activity, and economic regionalism may be an important means of such economies achieving a more self-sustaining pattern of growth.

In the next chapter I shall consider the problems faced by small underdeveloped countries attempting to accelerate their rate of economic growth under contemporary conditions, contrast their situation with the now developed small countries, outline the various advantages and disadvantages of size, and discuss the alternative strategies of development open to small countries.

CHAPTER II: UNDERDEVELOPMENT AND SELF-SUSTAINED GROWTH IN SMALL COUNTRIES

I DEVOTED the first chapter to an analysis of the concepts of underdevelopment, development, and self-sustained growth primarily in order to illustrate as sharply as possible the patterns of development open to a country very small in terms of both population and land area. For I believe that the alternatives open to small countries in the contemporary world are much more narrowly circumscribed than those open to larger countries. The underdeveloped countries are often lumped together in both academic and popular discussion. Moreover, as I have indicated, so much theorizing about growth either explicitly or implicitly assumes a large closed economy model that it is important for the student and the policy-maker alike to differentiate sharply between the growth process in a large closed economy and in a small open economy. In fact this has been my principal reason for focusing the theme of this book on the special case of development in small countries.

It is only recently that economists have begun to pay some attention to the economics of size. The interest was first sparked off in the mid-1950's by the beginning of the great debate on European economic integration which is still continuing. More recently interest has been generated in the topic for a different set of reasons. This is the emergence to independent sovereign nationhood of a large number of small countries in the Caribbean, in South East Asia, and in West and Equatorial Africa. Although some efforts have been made—notably the 1957 Symposium of the International Economic Association[1] and

[1] E. A. G. Robinson, ed., *Economic Consequences of the Size of Nations*, London, 1960, especially Kuznet's article on 'The Economic Growth of Small Nations'.

Sidney Dell's recent book[2]—the field is still open for further exploration of the wide-ranging issues raised by the relationship between size and economic development.

It is clear that in the past size has not presented any insuperable obstacles to economic growth. Witness the present economic strength of many small countries such as Switzerland (5½ million people in 1961), Luxembourg (300,000), Belgium (9 million), Holland (11½ million), Denmark (4½ million), New Zealand (2½ million), Norway (3½ million), and Sweden (7½ million).

My contention, however, is that these countries were able to develop at the time they did because the world environment was different from what it is today and that the contemporary situation faced by today's small underdeveloped countries is different in many essential respects from what it was 150, 100, or even 50 years ago. At the same time it is obvious that, if only because of the previous success stories, small size *per se* has some obvious advantages as well as disadvantages for development.

In this chapter I shall therefore consider the problems of very small countries attempting to accelerate (or maintain) their rate of economic growth in the conditions of the contemporary world and contrast their situation not only with the now developed small countries but also with the very large underdeveloped ones. I shall also outline the various advantages and disadvantages of size and suggest alternative strategies of development.

In the previous chapter I defined a small country as one with a population of 5 million or less and with usable land area of 10 to 20 thousand square miles or less. While others have defined a small country less restrictively, it should be borne in mind that Sidney Dell has pointed out that out of 112 countries or territories classified by the U.N. as underdeveloped, no fewer than 91 have a population of less than 15 million and 65 have less than 5 million.[3] I come from a part of the world where very few of the national economies have more than ½ million people. Even the now defunct West Indies Federation

[2] Sidney Dell, *Trade Blocs and Common Markets*, New York, 1963.
[3] Dell, p. 218.

had a population of only 3 million—so that the separate Caribbean economies may be considered as very small indeed. On this definition countries like China, India, Pakistan, and Brazil would be regarded as big in terms of both population and usable land area, while countries like the Caribbean Islands and territories, Cyprus, Malta, the Central American Republics, and many of the new States of Africa (especially the former colonies of France) would be regarded as small. And among the developed countries there is an obvious contrast between the U.S.A. and the U.S.S.R. on the one hand and Iceland, Denmark, Holland, Luxembourg, and New Zealand on the other.

This is all of course very arbitrary; but quite obviously there can be no absolute hard and fast line between a big and small country, between a closed and open economy, between a continental and small island economy. At the extremes the distinction is clear enough, say India and Malta; but then there is the large number of underdeveloped countries with a population of 10 to 60 million people and a land area which is far from being continental in size. I refer to such countries as Argentina, Mexico, Nigeria, and Burma, all with populations ranging from 20 to 55 million. And as we saw in the first chapter, Australia and Canada occupy a peculiar position in that they are both quite definitely continental in size but relatively small in population. In the real world judgments based on common sense often have to be substituted for the more rigorous categories of pure analysis. Accordingly, while I shall conduct most of my analysis in terms of ideal types, the obvious point should be borne in mind that ideal types seldom correspond to observable categories in the real world, except in extreme situations, such as India and Malta, Pakistan and Barbados, the U.S.A. and Luxembourg. Analysis always means simplification. Theory always caricatures reality.

Albert Hirschman has recently reminded us that we sometimes make too much of the dichotomy between developed and underdeveloped countries and that there are substantial differences, and even possible conflicts of interests, between different groups of underdeveloped countries. He instanced the difficulties faced by 'older' textile exporters such as India through the establishment of protected industries producing the same commodity in 'newer' countries such as Africa.[4] I would like to suggest that the study of development could be enriched if we made a distinction between 'large' and 'small' underdeveloped countries.

It may be objected that a definition of size purely in terms of population and land area omits two very important dimensions of the phenomenon. The first of these dimensions is *per capita* income which, when combined with numbers of population, gives aggregate purchasing power. The second dimension of size is access to foreign markets.

My answer to the first objection is that, while *per capita* income is a good measure of welfare, aggregate income is more relevant to a wide range of development problems. The two variables—numbers and *per capita* income—are not really quite analogous to Marshall's two blades of the scissors. I hope to develop this point at a later stage.[5]

Secondly, while I concede that the total market for a country's goods must of course include foreign as well as domestic purchases, the extension of the domestic market through developing exports is precisely the major problem facing most of the small underdeveloped countries today.

At this stage I should like to get out of the way certain quite obvious points. In attempting to analyse the economics of size,

[4] A. Hirschman, 'Comments on Papers Dealing with Comparative Costs and Economic Development', *Proceedings of the American Economic Association, December 1963* in *American Economic Review*, May 1964, pp. 426–8.

[5] Apart from total population and *per capita* income, there are, of course, two other factors which affect the size of the internal market for goods—both being unfavourable. One is internal transport costs and the other is the share of subsistence output in total income. It is obvious that for any given level of aggregate income in a country, the domestic market for goods will be smaller, the higher are internal transport costs and the greater the value of subsistence production relatively to cash transactions. A country which has a large total purchasing power but which is sparsely populated can have a unified national market only at the cost of very heavy investment in transport facilities.

I am not overlooking the eternal verities of economic development which hold irrespective of the size of the country, its degree of participation in foreign trade, or its relative emphasis on the role of the public and private sectors. In any economy development is facilitated by certain attitudes such as a high propensity to save, hard work, readiness to invest and to innovate; by institutions such as a well-developed capital market and an agrarian system which provides incentives for increasing agricultural productivity; and by the pursuit of appropriate monetary, fiscal, and other economic policies. Above all, large and small countries alike can suffer from certain structural constraints to economic development, the most important of which may be an unfavourable *ratio* between population on the one hand and the stock of capital and natural resources on the other hand. In terms of this Malthusian constraint large countries such as India and China are in the same position as the small overpopulated islands of the Caribbean.

In this chapter I am merely following the time-honoured technique of partial equilibrium analysis. Holding everything else constant under the umbrella of *ceteris paribus*, I shall concentrate only on two variables which I consider strategic to the growth process but which in my view have been neglected, namely absolute size of population and absolute amount of usable land area. I shall not be considering the *ratio* between population and land area, i.e. the Malthusian constraint.

Let me begin the discussion of the economics of size by contrasting the pattern of development in a large continental economy with that of a very small country.

The continental country, as we saw in the previous chapter, is likely to have a very wide range of resources including tropical agriculture, semi-temperate agriculture and, much more important, natural resources and raw materials ranging from hydroelectric potential to iron ore, coal, petroleum, and non-ferrous metals.

Therefore such a country will be perfectly justified in seeking to achieve a balanced structure of domestic production involving the building up of heavy industry and the whole range of consumer goods, intermediate products, and finished capital goods. However, in the process of achieving this balanced structure it will experience two conceptually distinct problems of finding resources. The first is that of mobilizing sufficient domestic savings to finance the desired level of investment. The second is that of securing specific foreign inputs to fill in the gaps still remaining in the domestic structure of production. In other words there is a savings-investment problem and there is a foreign exchange problem. In Mrs. Joan Robinson's terminology the 'foreign exchange barrier' is not the same as the 'inflation barrier'.[6] For, leaving aside for the time being the possibility of expanding exports, even if the country could mobilize enough domestic resources by non-inflationary means to finance its investment programme, it might still face a severe foreign exchange problem arising from the impossibility of producing domestically certain specific items, in practice principally certain specific intermediate and capital goods.

It is not too difficult to see that in such a situation efforts to achieve an *ex-ante* balance between required savings and desired investment could be self-defeating in that national income could fall either through domestic deflation or a loss of real output, if the required foreign exchange to secure the specific imported goods is not forthcoming. Even if additional domestic resources are mobilized for investment by cutting real consumption through inflationary finance, the problem would re-

[6] Cf. I. G. Patel, 'Trade and Payments Policy for a Developing Economy', *International Trade Theory in a Developing World*, London, 1963, p. 310. Also, J. P. Lewis, *Quiet Crisis in India*, New York, 1964, pp. 40–1; and W. Reddaway, *The Development of the Indian Economy*, Illinois, 1962, Appendix X, pp. 212–16. On the other hand G. E. Maier in his *International Trade and Development*, New York, 1963, takes the orthodox line that the savings-investment constraint and the foreign exchange constraint in developing countries are one and the same thing (see Chapter 4 on 'External Balance'). The condition under which the two constraints are the same can be stated formally as follows: the marginal import-content of domestic consumption must be equal to the marginal import-content of domestic investment. When the latter exceeds the former, which is almost bound to occur in a country which does not have a large capital goods sector, an increase in domestic investment cannot be achieved merely by increasing domestic savings.

main. In fact in such a situation there would be a strain on the foreign balance both because aggregate expenditure exceeds aggregate resources and because of the specificity of imported inputs. If, following the practice of the developed countries in time of war, a 'disequilibrium system' is attempted (i.e. the use of price controls, rationing, import and exchange controls in order to suppress the effects of inflationary finance), the foreign exchange problem in respect of the specific inputs would still remain. The problem of mobilizing domestic resources could always be solved through high taxation, high voluntary savings or deficit finance; but the balance-of-payments disequilibrium would still remain.

Now the classic way in which an economy in this situation gets hold of the foreign exchange required for the purchase from abroad of the specific inputs is through developing exports—either export staples or manufactured goods. In the contemporary world many underdeveloped countries find it difficult if not impossible to do this because of income—and price— in elastic demand conditions for tropical foodstuffs, raw materials, and light manufactured goods or because restrictive commercial policies in the advanced countries do not permit of real comparative advantages in manufactured goods being realized.[7] There is of course always the possibility of a high *price*-elasticity of demand for a particular export commodity of a particular country; but where the country is very large and

[7] The difficulties of expanding exports of primary products and of light labour-intensive goods (even at constant terms of trade) have by now been well documented. See for example the G.A.T.T. *Report by a Panel of Experts on Trends in World Trade*, Geneva, 1958, and United Nations, 'Towards a New Trade Policy', *Report by the Secretary-General of the U.N. Conference on Trade and Development*, New York, 1964. Dudley Seers has also given a theoretical analysis of the problem in his 'A Model of Comparative Rates of Growth of the World Economy', *Economic Journal*, June 1962. It was this gloomy outlook for exports of many primary products that led Nurkse to formulate his concept of 'incremental comparative advantage' as distinct from 'established comparative advantage', implying that a primary-producing country might be well advised to put new or incremental resources into investment in manufacturing industries. See his *Patterns of Trade and Development*, Stockholm, 1959.

45

produces a large proportion of world exports of the commodity, this may hardly be a possibility open to it.

But, more fundamentally, even if it were possible to realize the static gains from trade at any moment of time through a higher volume of exports of agricultural products or light labour-intensive manufactured consumer goods, this might divert real resources from the building up of a balanced structure of production and so postpone the advent of self-sustained growth. A balanced structure of production will in the end solve the balance-of-payments problem of the country but, paradoxically, the process of achieving this goal puts severe pressure on the balance of payments. This is the rationale of aid to help finance (i.e. to provide foreign exchange for) the takeoff in a large continental economy. In this situation foreign resources (whether in the form of aid or trade) have a 'balancing' function, balancing the demand for and the supply of specific inputs.

Yet it must be conceded that in this type of economy it is still possible to pursue the alternative strategy which makes exports more of a 'leading' sector; and these exports can be either traditional primary products or light labour-intensive manufactures, or an appropriate combination of the two types of commodities. For example, the country may deliberately decide to reduce its exchange rate in order to increase export earnings, in the event that price-elasticities of supply and demand make this feasible, even if it thereby worsens its terms of trade. In actual fact for a continental economy there could be a number of possible gradations of development strategy between the extremes of pure export-stimulation and pure import-substitution.

For my part, I am absolutely convinced that the balanced pattern of development is the correct one for large continental countries such as India and others to follow, having regard to population pressure, the varied natural and physical resources, and the demand conditions facing their exports in world markets. I also have a great deal of sympathy for the enormous economic problems facing the Indian sub-continent and a great deal of admiration for the resolute and intelligent way in which the governments and peoples of India and Pakistan are attempting to solve their problems.

But at the same time I cannot help feeling that the continental pattern of development has not been distinguished sharply enough from the patterns of development open to the very small underdeveloped countries and that as a result the problems faced by the small countries have been obscured.

We have seen that foreign transactions (aid and exports) in the continental economy attempting a takeoff through building up a rounded structure of production have a 'balancing' function. By this I do not refer to the trivial proposition taken from the definitional identities of national income accounting that *ex-post* the value of Aggregate Supply (i.e. the G.D.P. plus Imports) must be equal to the value of Aggregate Demand (i.e. Consumption plus Investment plus Exports). By the balancing role of foreign transactions I mean something much more fundamental—the literal filling-in of the gaps left in the structure of production. This should not be taken as denying the important role of foreign trade even in countries with such a development strategy in improving the allocation of resources along the lines of comparative advantage. It is even quite possible that, as Arthur Lewis[8] and others have argued, India's long-run comparative advantage in foreign trade lies in the export of capital goods in exchange for agricultural products.

On the other hand, the role of foreign trade in the long-run strategy of development of a small island economy is essentially different. As we have seen in the first chapter, a small country's resources are likely to be highly skewed as compared with those of a larger one. This being the case, although, as we have already seen, the volume of inter-industry transactions (i.e. the making of intermediate and capital goods) increases with economic development (properly conceived of as transformation of the economic structure), the process of filling in the boxes in an input-output table containing any given number of boxes stops sooner for any given level of *per capita* income than in a larger and more diversified economy. Further, economies of scale can

[8] W. A. Lewis, 'Economic Development with Unlimited Supplies of Labour', *Manchester School*, May 1954, pp. 139–91.

often not be achieved on the basis of producing only for the domestic market.[9] Specialization is much greater in a small country, the domestic structure of production differing quite sharply from the domestic composition of final demand. The consequence of this state of affairs is that, while the macro-economic relations between production, absorption and foreign trade hold good in a trivial sense and while foreign trade serves the role of matching the structure of production with the composition of final demand, the role of exports is much more that of a leading sector in the sense that the rate of growth of the G.D.P. is tied much more closely to the rate of growth of exports than in a very large economy. It is the growth of external demand which causes the economy to move. In the case of India while sluggish demand for exports can lead to difficulties in financing (in a real sense) the takeoff, the rate of growth of demand for exports does not impose the same long-run constraints on the rate of growth of domestic production. In other words import-substitution (potential and actual) is at the heart of India's development strategy, even if during the takeoff the lag in exports may create profound balance-of-payments difficulties. In a small country, however, the constraint imposed on growth by the external sector is a continuing phenomenon. In India the foreign exchange constraint is essentially a transitory phenomenon of the takeoff period. It may last for ten or even twenty years. In a very small country the constraint, if not the poor, will be with it for ever. It is a permanent fact of the national economy.

[9] I must here observe that, while the concept of economies of scale is perhaps among the most overworked tools in economic analysis and while the existence of the phenomenon has certainly been established in the real world (ask any businessman), surprisingly little empirical work has been done in order to establish its incidence from industry to industry. The International Co-operation Administration (now the Agency for International Development) has done some solid work on the subject in connection with the measurement of 'break-even' points of plants in different industries. The U.N. Centre for Industrial Development is also doing work on the subject. For a good review of some of the empirical evidence, see Bela Belassa, *The Theory of Economic Integration*, Illinois, 1961, Chapter 6.

The leading examples of export-led transformation in the contemporary world are Puerto Rico and Hong Kong, while the classic examples of a strategy based on import-substitution are India and Brazil. In the case of Puerto Rico exports have been growing faster than Gross National Product since the initiation of its industrial development programme.[10] Similarly, in the U.K. the foreign trade ratio increased in the first half of the nineteenth century.[11] This situation is probably associated with a rising volume of imported raw materials to which value is added locally before they are shipped out again. But in small dependent economies such as Puerto Rico with no monetary autonomy it may equally be due to a failure of domestic expenditure to grow as fast as the increase in exports warranted. We shall return to this point below.

This is of course a somewhat stark depiction of the problem. To the extent that domestic agricultural production has been lagging behind the growth of demand for food in a very small economy, it is quite feasible for growth to take place on the basis of import-substitution of locally produced for imported food. Within certain limits, too, growth need not be entirely led by exports in small countries suffering from heavy structural unemployment. Under certain conditions, the construction sector, the output of which is entirely 'non-tradeable', could assume a more propulsive role in such economies. The experience of Hong Kong,[12] and to a lesser extent of Jamaica in the 1950's, illustrates this. We shall develop this point below when we come to consider the precise degree of openness of the economy at which policy-makers in small countries should aim.

It is also possible for such an economy to build up a limited range of consumer-goods industries on the basis of production for the home market, i.e. import-substitution. The process of

[10] Werner Baer, 'Puerto Rico: An Evaluation of a Successful Development Programme', *Quarterly Journal of Economics*, LXXIII, 1959. See also J. E. Haring, 'External Trade as an Engine of Growth', *Economia Internazionale*, XIV, 1961.

[11] Kindleberger, *Foreign Trade*, p. 180.

[12] On Hong Kong, see E. Szcepanik, *The Economic Growth of Hong Kong*, London, 1958.

import-substitution in consumer goods can, as we have seen, take place without protection; but the process has generally been assisted both historically and in the contemporary world by protection. The rise of local industry figures prominently in the work of the location theorists, and the economic historian, North, has shown how the expansion of the export base in a regional economy within the continental economy of the U.S.A. has led to the development of local 'residentiary' or market-oriented consumer goods industries without the benefit of tariff protection or special inducements.[13] It is also possible that the growth of consumer incomes through the expansion of the export base can lead to the development of a limited range of intermediate goods, such as cement, wood, bricks, and other building materials.

It should however be pointed out that these 'residentiary' consumer goods industries and this limited range of inter-mediate goods are heavily protected by transport costs. For this reason alone one would expect sharp limits to the process of import-substitution. Then there is the further question of economies of scale. Here the situation would be even less favourable with regard to many classes of intermediate pro-ducts and capital goods, since economies of scale and a bal-anced availability of natural resources are more important in these than in consumer goods industries.

This *a priori* reasoning has been confirmed by the brilliant researches of Hollis Chenery. Chenery in a pathbreaking article[14] set out to answer the following question: what are the factors behind the growth of individual sectors of manufactur-ing industry in the course of economic development? Very briefly, his conclusions, arrived at after an econometric study using cross-section data for some fifty countries, both indus-trialized and non-industrialized, are:

1. There is a strong correlation between industrialization and the level of *per capita* income.

[13] Douglas North, 'Location Theory and Regional Economic Growth', *Journal of Political Economy*, June 1955, pp. 243–58.

[14] H. B. Chenery, 'Patterns of Industrial Growth', *American Economic Review*, September 1960.

2. There is also a strong correlation between the level of income and the type of industry.

3. The major source of growth in industrial production is import-substitution.

4. Only a minor part of growth in industrial production is to be explained by import-substitution in consumer-goods industries arising from income-elasticity with growing *per capita* incomes.

5. The major source of growth is import-substitution in industrial production in respect of intermediate and capital goods.

6. The effect of the size of a country is smallest in respect of services, agriculture, and most consumer goods and greatest for industries such as machinery, transport equipment, and intermediate products.

To the extent that Chenery's results are even approximately correct, some rather disturbing corollaries arise for small countries.

These corollaries are exceptionally disturbing for a very small country, defined as one with less than, say, three million people. For however high its *per capita* income may be (due to, say, the export of resource products on favourable terms), its very small absolute size of population imposes sharp limits on the extent to which it can economically produce intermediate and capital goods for the home market. It is true that in a small country with a high *per capita* income the demand for final manufactured goods for the home market may be higher than in an economy with twice the population but with one-half the *per capita* income, because of the relatively high income-elasticity of demand for manufactures as compared with food-stuffs. Moreover, to the extent that higher *per capita* incomes are correlated with greater equality in income-distribution, the domestic market for consumer goods will be bigger in the country with the smaller population but the higher *per capita* income. But, on the other hand, the higher the *per capita* income and hence the greater the share of income-elastic goods in domestic final demand, the more variety in style and design might be required, while in a country with a lower *per capita* income there would be less demand for variety in style and design. In the more populous but poorer countries, therefore, the realization of economies of scale would be more feasible. Accordingly the scales are rather finely balanced when it comes to respective advantages in producing consumer goods.

This relates to consumer goods. But when we take account of intermediate and capital goods the balance of advantage in favour of the larger country becomes much more clear-cut for the following reasons: (1) the greater scope for economies of scale in these products; (2) the more varied pattern of resources making possible the domestic production of more basic inputs; and (3) the higher elasticity of production of intermediate and capital goods with respect to the growth of G.D.P. as compared with consumer goods. Let us take two concrete examples to illustrate the point. It is much easier for India to produce steel and machinery than Mauritius because India has deposits of iron ore and coal, whereas Mauritius has neither. Again, quite apart from the provenance of the inputs, India can produce railway lines more economically for her home market than can Mauritius, in spite of the higher *per capita* income of Mauritius, because the territory of India covers millions of square miles over which the railway lines can run. In neither of the two cases is India's ability to produce economically dependent upon her level of *per capita* income which, as everyone knows, is exiguous.[15]

Looking at the pure *economics* of the matter and leaving aside the political instruments used and the all-pervading role of the state, the pattern of development in a large continental country here described bears many similarities to that followed by the U.S.S.R. from the inception of the Five-Year Plans in 1928.

[15] W. A. Lewis has described the limitations of a country with a small population very well. He says: 'We also have the paradox that a country may be overpopulated relatively to its agricultural resources, but underpopulated relatively to its capacities for industrial development. Some very small countries, like Jamaica or Mauritius, face the problem that their populations are much too large in relation to agriculture, and at the same time much too small to support a wide range of industrial development.' W. A. Lewis, *Theory of Economic Growth*, London, 1955, p. 324.

Here the attempt was made to build up a 'rounded' structure of production containing all 'stages' of production from heavy industry (i.e. capital and intermediate goods) to consumer-goods industries. It is true that the Soviet Union placed great emphasis on capital goods and too little on consumer goods and housing, and failed to increase significantly agricultural productivity either per acre or per man, but its rationale was, broadly speaking, an attempt at a 'rounded' structure of production, especially with respect to the industrial sector. It is clear that this pattern is one that is feasible only in a large continental country where there is a rounded availability of natural resources and a large enough population to provide economies of scale.[16]

The Soviet pattern is a 'model' prescribing a particular policy. But there are other more formal post-Keynesian growth-models pitched at a much higher level of abstraction and designed to illuminate under restrictive assumptions the relationships between economic variables in the course of economic growth. Even at the level of abstraction on which they are set, many of these two-sector models dividing the economy into a capital-goods and a consumer-goods sector cannot directly illuminate economic relationships in most of the world's countries which are small and have no capital-goods sector. Even as theoretical constructs they are irrelevant to the realities of these countries. It would be an interesting exercise for those

[16] A lucid rationalization of the Soviet model of development is given in Maurice Dobb's recent *Economic Growth and Underdeveloped Countries*, London, 1963. To be fair to Dobb, he recognizes in one of the last paragraphs that the size of a country limits the general applicability of his model. See Dobb, pp. 57–8. In this connection it is most interesting to observe that the new régime in Cuba at first attempted a strategy of industrialization similar to the Soviet pattern: import-substitution with emphasis on basic industries as against consumer goods, in spite of a population of only 7 million and a deficiency of sources of energy. See Dudley Seers, ed., *Cuba: The Economic and Social Revolution*, Chapel Hill, 1964, pp. 326–38. However, towards the end of 1963 the strategy was modified and emphasis shifted to the utilization of domestic raw materials as the basis for exports of manufactures. See 'The New Cuban Industrial Policy', *The World Today*, September 1963, pp. 371–4.

with an interest in model-building to attempt to 'translate' some of these models into terms of a small open economy. For 'capital-goods producing sector' they would certainly have to write 'earnings of export sector adjusted for changes in the commodity terms of trade' or what the Latin Americans call 'the capacity to import'. But it is obviously much more important that efforts should be made to develop models consciously designed to illustrate the working of a small open economy. Dudley Seers has made the pioneering attempt,[17] about which I shall say more presently.

We may further contrast the situation between a large continental country and a small one in terms of the applicability of the doctrine of balanced growth in the more technical sense which the term has acquired in the literature of economic growth. That is to say, we shall for the moment abandon the meaning which I gave the term a few moments ago to refer to a situation where the domestic structure of production matches the domestic composition of final demand.

We shall consider the applicability to small countries of the three principal versions of the balanced-growth doctrine—those of Lewis, Rosenstein-Rodan, and Nurkse.

Lewis' doctrine[18] of balanced growth is simplicity itself and, indeed, it almost amounts to a tautological statement of the requirements of balance in the national accounting sense. Lewis distinguishes between three sectors: manufacturing for the home market, agricultural production for the home market, and exports. According to his conception, *given the rate of growth of exports*, manufacturing and agricultural production must expand at rates, not necessarily identical, but corresponding to their respective income-elasticities of demand. If agricultural production does not grow at an appropriate rate, either the internal commodity terms of trade between agriculture and manufacturing will move in favour of agriculture, thus checking the expansion of the manufacturing sector, or the balance of payments will deteriorate through the rise in the demand for

[17] Dudley Seers, 'The Mechanism of an Open Petroleum Economy', *Social and Economic Studies*, June 1964.
[18] Lewis, *Theory of Economic Growth*, pp. 274-83.

food imports. It is obvious that this general proposition applies to both large and small countries since the national accounting arithmetic on which it rests must be true of any kind of economy, irrespective of its size or its degree of openness.

I therefore believe that it is difficult to quarrel with Lewis' formulation, since it applies to any economy, whatever its degree of openness. The other two versions are, however, different kettles of fish. They can be criticized on the grounds that they assume unlimited supplies of factors of production, especially capital and entrepreneurship; but, leaving aside these strictures, I still think that they are of limited applicability to very small economies.[19]

Rosenstein-Rodan rests his argument for a 'big push' method of transformation[20] on the grounds of complementarities and external economies in the supply of goods. These complementarities exist horizontally between industries at the same stage of production and vertically between different stages of production. His prescription is that planned advance should be made simultaneously on a large number of fronts to make investment profitable by capturing externalities. In his view, 'all industries are basic', each providing pecuniary external economies for the others.

If Rosenstein-Rodan approaches balance more from the side of supply, Nurkse emphasizes complementarities between different industries on the demand side. According to his version[21] insufficiency of real demand can inhibit economic

---

[19] It should, however, be pointed out that Hirschman, the champion of unbalanced growth, dismisses even the Lewis version of the doctrine on the ground that, the development process being a chain of disequilibria, a prescription in terms of 'retrospective comparative statics' such as the Lewis version is irrelevant. See Hirschman, *The Strategy of Economic Development*, pp. 62–5. In spite of this, I consider the Lewis rule of thumb a useful guide to economic programmers.

[20] P.N. Rosenstein-Rodan, 'Notes on the Theory of the "Big Push" ', *Economic Development for Latin America*, ed. by H. S. Ellis, reproduced in Morgan, Betz and Choudry, *Readings in Economic Development*, California, 1963.

[21] R. Nurkse, *Problem of Capital Formation in Underdeveloped Countries*, Oxford, 1958.

growth in that the product of one industry started in isolation may not be absorbed domestically since those who earn factor incomes in the single industry will hardly spend their entire incomes on the products of the single industry. Adequate real demand will be forthcoming only if a sufficiently large number of industries is established at one and the same time, so that they will all provide markets for each other.

Whatever may be their merits or demerits as applied to large countries, the Nurkse and Rosenstein-Rodan doctrines can hardly be applied to very small countries where economies of scale and lack of variety of resources will preclude the simultaneous establishment of a large number of industries all producing for the domestic market.

As we shall see presently, these doctrines can be of some applicability to small underdeveloped countries only in the context of economic integration, where the integrated area is large both geographically and in terms of population. On the basis of such a large economically integrated area, it might be possible to reap the benefits of externalities on the side of supply and demand.

The doctrines of balanced growth à la Nurkse and Rosenstein-Rodan can of course be attacked on the grounds that they do not envisage the widening of the market through the development of export industries. This brings us at last to the crucially important factor in the industrial development of small countries, namely the finding of export markets.

But before we discuss this, let us explore further some of the implications for small countries of economies of scale. First, it is easy to say that research should be carried out on adapting technology to the requirements of small markets. But such research will take a very long time to bear fruit. And indeed it is doubtful whether one will ever find any such techniques which are efficient.

Second, an attempt may be made to set up either plants of sub-optimum size or optimum-sized plants operating below the most efficient point, the latter situation involving excess capacity. In both situations costs and prices are likely to be high. And tariffs and other trade restrictions will be so high that real income may even fall, although this will be counterbalanced by greater employment opportunities. This is of course a rather dangerous solution of the problem and hardly a practicable one.

Third, it has been argued that economies of scale apply only to manufacturing production and that therefore the disadvantages of small size are confined to only one sector of the economy. This would not matter so much were not manufacturing production a key sector of the economy. For if we divide the economy into a goods-producing and a service-producing sector, it is clear that it is the goods-producing sector which gives the service sector its forward impetus.[22] As we have seen, manufacturing usually grows faster than agriculture in the course of transformation, so that the emergence of a large manufacturing sector is in most cases the strategic element in growth. Economies of scale therefore adversely affect small countries at their most strategic point.

Next, there may well be significant economies of scale in basic governmental administration for countries above a certain very small size. It is difficult to substantiate this point empirically[23] but one feels that for a country with less than three million people, the full economies of scale of basic governmental administration services may not be realized. And, apart from strictly administrative services, there may also be economies of scale in the operation of certain public utilities, in particular railways, telephones, and water systems.

Finally, there is the question of monopolies. The small size of the home market, combined with economies of scale, makes monopoly or oligopoly positions almost inevitable in very small countries. But to the extent that the country does not give excessive protection to these industries, their monopoly power may be limited by the availability of imports.

[22] Compare W. Galenson, 'Economic Development and the Sectoral Expansion of Employment', *International Labour Review*, June 1 1963, pp. 1–15.

[23] Compare the Chapters 14 and 15 on 'Cost of Administration' in Robinson, ed., *Economic Consequences of the Size of Nations*; also the Editor's Introduction, p. xxi.

It should not however be thought that in very large countries the realization of economies of scale is automatic. Even where the domestic market is large enough to support a few plants of optimum size, there may still exist an excessive number of plants of sub-optimum size. There may be several reasons for this. First of all, the domestic market may be fragmented by high transport costs or inadequate transportation facilities. Second, the government may be pursuing a conscious social policy of dispersal of industries in the interests of 'balanced' regional development. Or, third, the aim may be to prevent a concentration of economic power likely to result from the dominance of one or two large firms.[24]

The process of import-substitution in large countries will also experience further vicissitudes. The first is excess capacity arising from the desire on the part of entrepreneurs to install capacity ahead of the growth of demand. The result is of course high unit costs. Excess capacity is now very prevalent in Latin America, especially in the three largest countries, Brazil, Mexico, and Argentina.[25] The second is that in many countries import-substitution may already have reached its limits and the process of industrialization is likely to be aborted unless export markets can be developed.[26] But, third, although it is often claimed that a large home market is required as a base for exports, it is difficult to effect a rapid expansion of exports in an industrial structure established on the basis of import-substitution.[27]

[24] The last two reasons seem to be operative in India. See W. Malenbaum, 'Comparative Costs and Economic Development: The Experience of India', *Proceedings of the American Economic Association December 1963*, in *American Economic Review*, May 1964, pp. 390–9. But for a somewhat different point of view on India's industrial location policies, see J. P. Lewis, pp. 181–218.

[25] United Nations Centre for Industrial Development, *Trade in Manufactures and Semi-Manufactures*, mimeographed paper prepared for the U.N. Conference on Trade and Development, February 1964, para. 40.

[26] Ibid.

[27] Compare Hirschman, *Proceedings of the American Economic Association, December 1963*, p. 427.

Again, we should be careful not to press the disadvantages of small scale too far. First of all, even where economies of scale do not matter, countries can still be high-cost and inefficient producers. The blame for high-cost production should not always be laid entirely at the door of economies of scale.[28] The fault may not always lie in the size of small countries, but in themselves.

Further, even in fairly small countries, it may be feasible to manufacture not only consumer goods which are market-oriented, such as beer, aerated beverages, confectionery, and cigarettes. Certain 'intermediates' such as cement, bricks, and building materials are, as we have seen, location oriented, by reason of heavy transport costs, both by land and sea.[29] And the development of technology and the reduction of transport costs in recent years have made it possible to manufacture certain elementary types of steel on a relatively small scale using imported iron ore and coal or locally available scrap. In other words, heavy transport costs put certain intermediates outside the range of tradeable goods and technology has in large part removed the resource constraint from steel production.

Even if it is conceded that small overpopulated countries have to export, it may also be argued that they do not necessarily have to export *manufactured* goods, but may export invisibles, such as tourism, international transport services (shipping and air travel), and financial services. This is a pertinent question, since formally as well as effectively exports of services are closely analogous to exports of manufactures, both being sources of external demand.

My general view is that for most small countries such sources of foreign exchange are likely to be a complement to, and not a substitute for, exports of manufactures. It is true that tourism is highly income-elastic, but it depends so largely on whim and fashion that it would not be prudent in countries where it is

[28] Compare W. Chudson (ibid., p. 407) who cites the example of the African textile industry.

[29] On the growth of production of intermediates in Puerto Rico, see Haring, 'External Trade'; and in Africa, Chudson, p. 406.

possible to develop manufactures to place hopes entirely or largely on this industry. For, while it is equally true that different kinds of manufactured exports are likely to experience changes in demand abroad, it is my contention that the creation of an industrial structure geared to exports in itself involves the development of a *capacity to transform*, that is to be adaptable, to be technologically dynamic, and to shift resources from one manufactured export to another in accordance with shifts in demand in external markets. In my judgment tourism does not develop the capacity to transform to the same extent. On the other hand, there may well be certain small countries which have great natural advantages for tourism and little for manufacturing industry, and in such places the concentration on tourism may be the only feasible alternative.

The development of earnings from international sea and air transport may make sense for a few small countries; but clearly if many such countries entered the field, the result could well be world excess capacity.

Again, not many small countries have the capacity or even the location to become important international financial centres; and it can even be argued that there are in the contemporary world only three important financial centres—New York, London, and Zurich. But it is conceivable that certain small countries which have political stability and a tradition of banking and finance could develop into financial centres for certain regions.

The role of invisible exports is therefore fairly limited in most small countries. This is clearly seen by considering the balance of payments of Switzerland, the classic home of invisible exports—tourism and financial services. In 1955 visible exports accounted for 70 per cent of the exports of all goods and services.[30]

Everything therefore points to a major concentration on efforts to develop exports of manufactures. But before we turn to an examination of the problems raised by this, we must

[30] Calculated from Johr's article on 'Size and Efficiency in Switzerland', Robinson, ed., *Economic Consequences of the Size of Nations*, p. 64; and from *U.N. National Accounts Year Book 1962*, p. 253.

examine further some of the advantages and disadvantages of small size, apart from the implications of the fundamental factors of lack of varied resources and lack of large internal markets which we have been examining under the general heading of economies of scale. These are the dependent character of growth process, the possible large dependence on foreign commercial investment, the consequences for employment and resource-mobilization of the openness of the economy, and the operation of the demonstration-effect *within* such countries.

First, and as a corollary of this fundamental disadvantage, even with transformation the character of growth cannot be as autonomous and as self-sustaining as in a large closed economy; for, since the continued growth of exports is necessary to keep the G.D.P. expanding, the growth of the G.D.P. in the long run depends on the momentum of external demand. The economy can only adjust to external vulnerability by being flexible, adaptable, and ready to introduce innovations, whether cost-reducing or product-introducing.

Second, a very small country which possesses a particular mineral or natural resource in large quantities which is developed by foreign capital may find that the enclave sector is so large relatively to the rest of the economy that the enclave can dominate the entire economy. This may be a good thing for raising *per capita* income; but in the extreme situation it may become impossible even to conceive of a separate national economy. All the important decisions about the economy will be taken by large international corporations and government and domestic producers alike will have very little real autonomy in determining the evolution of the economic life of the community. The economy becomes dependent in a very fundamental way. Another question which arises in this situation is the meaning of aggregates such as the G.D.P. and the rate of capital formation in such economies. The mineral-producing sector may be so large that the weight of other sectors in such aggregates may be very slight. In such economies there is a further question concerning the definition of 'national' savings. It has been argued that in such countries accruals to the depreciation funds of large foreign companies operating locally are not strictly speaking 'foreign investment' but are part of 'national savings' in that they are generated within the country almost automatically. In this conception it is only reinvested profits (and of course new investment from new funds) that should count as foreign investment. I do not accept this contention since, however permanently domiciled in the host country the foreign company may become, the decision to continue applying the depreciation funds to operations within the host country rests with an outside source.

Next, there are several consequences of the fact that structurally the economies of very small countries must remain very highly open in the sense that there must be a high percentage of exports and imports relatively to the Gross Domestic Product.

One may distinguish here between 'structural' and 'functional' openness.[31] By structural openness we mean simply that the economy by the mere factor of size must have a large volume of foreign transactions relatively to domestic transactions as compared with a country of the same level of *per capita* income but a larger population and a greater variety of resources, if transformation is to proceed. But, even within a narrow range determined by the structural factor of size, there is an area of choice left in terms of institutional mechanisms and policy operations. It is perhaps the supreme task facing those responsible for the management of such economies to recognize these limits and act accordingly. The problem is: given the vital dependence of the economy on an expansion of exports, on cheap imports, and on access to foreign private capital, how far should exchange controls and trade barriers be imposed and how far should monetary and financial practices and institutions depart from fully 'automatic' functioning in order that the authorities can be in a position to exercise more

[31] The distinction was pointed out to me by Mr. Alister McIntyre. See his forthcoming paper on *Decolonization and Trade Policy in the West Indies* to be published by the University of Puerto Rico. I am also indebted to Mr. McIntyre for very helpful discussion on the difficulty of mobilizing resources while maintaining the institutions of an open economy.

control over the local economy so as to mobilize more effectively local resources and to stimulate local production and local employment? In other words, to what extent should one seek to operate the 'disequilibrium system' in such economies and to what extent should one seek to pursue more active and less passive monetary, financial, and commercial policies?

It may be argued that there are three principal reasons for maintaining open monetary and financial institutions and for pursuing liberal and outward-looking trade and exchange control policies in small dependent economies. First, it is necessary that money costs of production be competitive so that exports can expand; and low money costs of production are clearly assisted by the absence of high tariffs and trade controls which keep down the cost of imported raw materials and capital goods and weaken incentives for wage increases by keeping down the cost of imported wage goods. There is also the stimulus to productive efficiency arising from the competition of cheap imports.

Second, the inflow of private capital is facilitated by monetary stability and an absence of exchange controls which allows the free remission of profits and capital in respect of foreign investment. Even when it might be considered justifiable to adopt the classical method of fostering exports—namely, a downward adjustment in the exchange rate—this may have to be completely ruled out because of the inhibiting effects on the future inflow of foreign investment.

Third, it is arguable that the absence of restrictions on commercial banks and other financial institutions may result in a large net inflow of foreign funds *via* such institutions, even though the decisions will rest with the overseas head offices of these institutions.

These considerations in favour of keeping a very small economy institutionally open have some cogency. But, where there is a large pool of structurally unemployed, the problem is that the promotion of employment and the mobilization of domestic financial resources may be hindered by such institutions and such practices.

Let us consider first the problem of resource mobilization.

63

Many small countries maintain fully convertible currencies rigidly pegged to important reserve currencies such as the dollar, the franc, or the pound sterling. When relative absence of exchange controls and the existence of a convertible currency are allied with the other institutions of a dependent economy such as the investment abroad of pension funds, life insurance funds, commercial bank deposits, and even government working balances, certain consequences follow.

There are several implications for resource mobilization. First, even if domestic savings are fairly high, much of these savings may be invested abroad and therefore not be available for domestic investment. In fact in many small countries with open economies and liberal trade and payments systems we often encounter the phenomenon of 'excess borrowing',[32] i.e. borrowing abroad and lending abroad at the same time. This is obviously quite an *uneconomic* procedure because most of the funds invested abroad will usually be placed in short-term assets carrying lower rates of interest than those paid on the long-term loans raised abroad.[33] Second, and more fundamentally, such heavy reliance on overseas funds means that the government of the small country has to present the right 'image' to the foreign investor, which may further reduce the possibility of the country pursuing even slightly unorthodox policies in order to mobilize domestic financial resources. The

[32] On the notion of excess borrowing which has a much broader connotation than that here used, see J. Knapp, 'Capital Exports and Growth', *Economic Journal*, September 1957.

[33] Professor Robert Mundell has pointed out to me that this is not necessarily uneconomic since the increase in foreign assets represents an increase in liquidity, or rather in the 'external money supply' which bears some definite relationship to economic activity, especially external transactions; and that the holding of money always has a cost. I do not accept this contention since not all the assets exported really remain as liquid balances available to the economy and since there is a clear loss to the economy on the interest rate differential. Professor Charles Kennedy has suggested that my strictures would not apply if the exported funds were invested in foreign equities which would probably earn more than the interest charges payable on long-term loans from abroad. To the extent that this would be feasible, I accept Kennedy's contention.

economy becomes open in much more than a technical sense and economic policies considered 'sound' by the foreign investor are pursued, irrespective of their real merits or their adequacy to the given situation. In extreme cases, the need to present the right image may even stand in the way of making fundamental diagnoses of the structural weaknesses of the economy or even publicizing temporarily adverse trends in economic indicators.

The difficulties of mobilizing domestic resources for development are further compounded by the absence of a broadly based capital market in such countries. Since the country is by definition very small, this means that there are relatively fewer transactions taking place in the capital and money markets than in larger countries, even those with much lower *per capita* incomes. In a small country a capital market confined to domestic transactions can never become as highly developed as in a larger country, unless indeed a small underdeveloped country becomes the Switzerland or New York of its geographical area; and this limitation on the development of capital markets further compounds the difficulties of mobilizing potential available domestic savings. In other words, not only is it difficult to ensure that such savings as may be generated in the local economy are locally invested; the savings ratio is smaller than it would be in the absence of a highly developed local capital market. The absence of such a highly developed capital market in turn is one of the reasons why local institutions and persons place their money abroad.

Finally, two further points should be brought out about monetary control in this kind of economy. The fundamental difficulty of insulation of the domestic economy from externally induced fluctuations through monetary policy derives from the 'structurally' determined openness of the economy. Exports may be so large in relation to domestic investment that a swing in export values could simply not be 'compensated' for by measures of domestic monetary expansion. But it should be further noted that, even apart from this fundamental factor, monetary control is difficult because of the nature of the commercial banking system (the local banks being branches of expatriate banks with head offices overseas) and because of the free flow of funds between the metropolitan and dependent country arising from free convertibility between the local and metropolitan currencies.

So far as concerns the mobilization of domestic financial resources, it should be noted that one may well sacrifice the effective mobilization of domestic savings to the hope of getting an inflow of foreign capital; and in fact, one might end up by getting the worse of both worlds, as abdication of efforts to mobilize domestic resources and the receipt of very little foreign capital. Moreover, in so far as the commercial banking system can finance an excess of domestic expenditure over domestic output by moving in funds from head office, the decision, as in all foreign borrowing, rests with individuals outside the national economy, in this case the people in the metropolitan head offices of the banks.

In fact, it is now generally accepted that there is a very good case for a move towards greater monetary and financial autonomy in small dependent open economies. While it is conceded that in these countries a central bank cannot do much to insulate the economy from declines in external demand, it is still felt that there is a positive role for such an institution in providing financial leadership and direction, in developing a local capital market and other financial institutions, and in selectively guiding the flow of credit to the various economic activities.

The employment problem arises from the fact that an automatic monetary system (similar to the Gold Standard) ties the rate of growth of domestic expenditure to that of exports. By checking the expansion of domestic expenditure, the expansion of employment is also restricted. And the lack of a balance-of-payments problem may under these circumstances merely be a reflection of inadequate employment and inadequate domestic demand. The problem is, however, complex since, as we have seen, the scope for a pattern of development dominated by import-substitution is restricted by limited opportunities for achieving economies of scale and by natural-resource constraints in small economies.

Assuming that trade is balanced and that there are no net capital movements and no net payments of profits abroad, one may in fact distinguish the pattern of development based on import-substitution in large closed economies from the pattern based on export-stimulation in small open economies in terms of the following simple algebra:

$$\frac{dY}{dt} > \frac{dX}{dt} \tag{1}$$

and

$$\frac{dY}{dt} \leqslant \frac{dX}{dt} \tag{2}$$

where $Y =$ Gross Domestic Product (which, by the assumption of no net capital movements $=$ Gross Domestic Expenditure),

$X =$ Exports (which, by the assumption of no net capital movements and no net payment of profits abroad $=$ Imports), and

$t =$ time

Equation (1) describes the import-substitution pattern of development, while equation (2) describes the process of development led by exports in a small open economy.[34]

The question is: how much scope is there for modifying the relationship expressed in equation (2) in small open economies? I believe there is some limited scope. For protection of local industry is not necessarily the only means of modifying the relationship between the rate of growth of domestic expenditure and the rate of growth of exports. I am of the view that in such economies the construction sector—especially housing (whose output is entirely non-tradeable)—could be made into a more propulsive sector of the economy. Analytically, there are two mechanisms for effecting this. One is a deliberate changing of consumption patterns away from imported goods either by voluntary individual decisions or by policy instru-

[34] This formulation was suggested by a somewhat similar one used for a different purpose by Dudley Seers in his analysis of the 'structural' factors in inflation in Latin America. See his, 'A Theory of Growth and Inflation', *Oxford Economic Papers*, May 1962.

ments. In this way there would be no strain on the balance of payments since there would be an autonomous shift from expenditure on imports to expenditure on housing. The alternative is some limited application of the disequilibrium system, involving the financing of construction expenditures through expansion in the money supply and some limited measure of controls to suppress inflationary pressures and to prevent a strain on the balance of payments. This would of course involve more autonomy in monetary management.

But, even after allowing for moves towards monetary autonomy and financial adaptation and for a consequent limited application of the disequilibrium system in order to give greater domestic control, to expand employment and to mobilize resources, it remains true that reasons of size, dependence on foreign trade and on foreign private capital inflows rule out the application of such a system in the extreme form often practised (with some justification) in many of the large and medium-sized countries. We may conclude that, as a general rule, deficit finance should never be allowed to go too far nor can trade and exchange controls ever become as severe or as all-pervasive as in larger countries whose strategies of development are based on import-substitution and whose need for a continuing expansion of exports may not be as critical. At the same time, this does not mean that small dependent economies should uncritically follow all the orthodox rules of the game as laid down by the advanced countries.

Another important implication of the structural openness of small economies is the relationship between wage rates and employment. An understanding of this relationship is of extreme importance to policy formulation in those small open economies which have a dual structure. This is because one of the results of trade-union activity is an attempt to generalize the relatively high wage rates paid by the modern highly productive sector to other sectors and industries which are less productive and therefore less able to afford to pay such high wages. In this situation it is not uncommon to find both trade-union leaders and various progressives rationalizing this state of affairs by arguing that to increase wage rates is to increase

68

purchasing power and therefore to widen the market for domestic production. Unfortunately the economic analyst, however progressive he may be, cannot take such a simple position.

I shall leave aside considerations of social justice and examine this doctrine. I believe that there are strict limits to its applicability in small open economies. The matter is very complex and cannot be fully discussed here, but I shall attempt to present an analysis based on a very brief and perhaps oversimplified set of arguments.

I assume across-the-board or fairly generalized increases in money wage rates, throughout the whole economy in the case of an industrial country, and throughout the modern sector in the case of an underdeveloped country.

Let me concede at once that a high level of domestic demand is essential in sustaining a high level of activity both in the short and in the long run in any exchange economy be it large or small, open or closed, developed or underdeveloped, centrally planned or governed by market forces. The real questions are three-fold. First, what are the best means of sustaining a high level of domestic demand? Second, are some methods of increasing domestic demand fraught with more harmful consequences than others? Third, to what extent and under what conditions will increases in supply be called forth in response to a high level of domestic demand?

There are, in principle, four principal ways in which an increase in demand could be generated:

1. an increase in productivity and so in real income in either the traditional or the modern sector or in both;

2. the expansion of employment in the modern sector of the economy at constant money wage rates and at constant productivity, so that average product per person and average real income is raised in both the modern and traditional sectors taken together, that is to say, in the whole economy. (This represents a 'widening of capital' in the modern sector as presented in the Arthur Lewis version of the classical model);

3. the inflationary financing of capital formation (i.e. deficit finance) without any increase in money wage rates for the

69

workers additionally employed in the investment projects;[35]

4. higher money wage rates for those already employed in the modern sector.

In this connection we have to distinguish between real and money demand. The first two mechanisms involve an increase in real demand, in that higher money incomes are generated *pari passu* with an increase in the supply of goods. On the other hand, the other two mechanisms involve an increase in money incomes without necessarily entailing concomitant increases in the supply of consumer goods.

Let us begin by distinguishing between three types of economies: developed industrial economies; large closed underdeveloped economies; and small open underdeveloped economies.

In the first case—developed economies—one must further distinguish between a situation of unemployment and one of full or near-full employment. In the first situation, there is, other things being equal, a presumption that an increase in money wage rates could on balance have favourable effects on recovery by increasing effective demand in accordance with the Keynesian model. On the other hand, in the second situation—full or near-full employment—increases in money incomes would encounter an inelastic supply of goods, since existing plant will be working at full or near-full capacity and inflationary pressures will tend to develop. In the somewhat longer run it is only through increases in productivity that inflationary pressures on the price level can be contained. But where money incomes per unit of output increase faster than productivity, there will be cost inflation; and, if the rate of increase in costs and prices is faster than that experienced by the country's trading partners, there will also be balance-of-payments pressures. The likelihood of balance-of-payments pressures emerging is greater, the more open is the economy of the industrialized country. It should, however, be noted that, apart from the likelihood of the emergence of balance-of-

[35] I ignore here the implications of the balanced budget multiplier theorem according to which an increase in government expenditure financed by an increase in tax revenue will increase aggregate demand.

payments problems, any tendency for wage rates to increase faster than productivity in industrial economies may not have adverse effects either on capital formation or on employment under a régime of 'administered prices' where the large oligo-polies can always increase prices by successfully adjusting their profit margins in the face of wage increases and where tax yields are highly sensitive to increases in money incomes. In other words, an attempt to redistribute real income away from entrepreneurs and government to workers purely through the wage mechanism will be abortive in such a situation, and one may have to rely instead on the fiscal mechanism to effect such a redistribution.

In the second case—large and relatively self-sufficient under-developed countries—the situation is akin to full employment or near-full employment in the developed industrial countries in that the short-run elasticity of supply is relatively low as compared with an unemployed industrial economy where both capital and labour are only temporarily underutilized during the slump. In an underdeveloped economy suffering from structural unemployment there is by definition an absence (in the short run, at least) of the factors of production which can co-operate with labour. These absent co-operant factors, it should be noted, include enterprise, skill, and organization as well as capital. In these circumstances, in the short period— before changes in productivity can manifest themselves—wage rises are clearly inflationary. And even when we allow for changes in productivity, the situation is also similar to that in a fully employed industrial economy in that wage increases in excess of productivity changes will lead to a situation of cost inflation.

However, these two results both depend on the assumption that entrepreneurs have sufficient market power to increase prices proportionately to wage increases. In other words it has been assumed that the market structure is such that income cannot be redistributed from entrepreneurs to workers. But, to the extent that the market structure can permit of such a re-distribution of income, economic activity may be stimulated in so far as workers have a higher propensity to spend than entrepreneurs. However, even if this is so, we have to take into account the longer run effects. These effects may be analysed under two heads.

First, rapidly rising wage rates may accelerate the introduction of more mechanized processes of production and to this extent employment will be adversely affected. On the other hand, some of the larger less developed countries may be in a stage of development where they can produce some, at least, of the capital goods which they may require and there will therefore be some compensation in so far as employment expands in the capital goods sector.

Second, there is the 'accumulation of capital' argument. In an industrial country or at near-full employment there is usually no great danger if wage rates increase exactly as fast as productivity. But in an underdeveloped country, it is desirable that wage increases should fall short of productivity increases so that the accumulation of surpluses for the continued expansion of output and employment in the modern sector of the economy can be maximized. This principle remains valid even if it is qualified by a recognition of the necessity to raise *per capita* real consumption because of the favourable effects on labour productivity of greater and more sustained effort from the workers. In any event, this qualification is applicable only in quasi-Malthusian conditions associated with extremely low levels of *per capita* incomes and living standards.

Apart, however, from the adverse effects of an increase in the share of the product going to workers on the rate of accumulation, increases in consumption could in the long run stimulate economic activity in such large economies if it is accompanied by a greater degree of import-substitution which, as we have seen, is the appropriate strategy of development in large economies. In other words, the Keynesian remedy could in a sense be made to work in the long run if there is a conscious policy of rapid import-substitution. Similar considerations apply to a controlled use of deficit finance in order to finance investment projects which would yield a supply of consumers' goods in a relatively short time.

In our third case—small open economies with a fixed rate of

exchange and an automatic monetary system—wage increases in the modern sector would not lead to much domestic inflation since the domestic price level is closely tied to that of exports and imports. Export prices are usually determined by world conditions, since the small country may not be an important supplier of the commodity. And, given the unrestricted availability of imports and their importance in domestic expenditure, import prices (over which the small country will also have little control) will have a very important influence on domestic prices. Moreover, because of the high marginal propensity to import both capital and consumer goods, a large part of increases in domestic incomes tends to spill over into a demand for imports. This means that in such economies a very large part of increases in money wages becomes automatically translated into an increase in real wages through more imports being pulled into the economy. And the combination of a high marginal propensity to import with an automatic monetary system further means that increases in money wages do not have much effect in increasing the demand for local goods and services and, hence, for local factors of production. In this kind of situation the balance of payments is kept in equilibrium at the expense of the expansion of domestic incomes and employment.

One might even go so far as to say that in this kind of economy a sort of 'wages fund' or, more accurately, a 'foreign exchange fund' exists in the short period. A very large part of any increase in money wages is *ipso facto* an increase in real wages, and such an increase in money wages may hinder the expansion of employment. This is because, given the import-function, there exists at any point in time a fixed amount of export income as well as foreign exchange which has to be divided up either between a smaller or larger number of workers.

Of course, some part of the increase in wages is spent locally since the marginal propensity to import is less than unity. There is, therefore, some increase in local purchasing power and, to the extent that the short period elasticity of supply is low, pressure would be exerted on the domestic price level.

73

One can say that a policy of import substitution could in the long run assist in making supply more elastic; but this raises the central problem besetting small economies—the range of feasible import substitution is narrowly circumscribed. It follows that even in the long run the proportion of total supply produced by the local economy cannot be very significant. The economy must look more to the expansion of external demand.

In any event, it seems better that domestic demand should be increased by using investment resources to expand employment opportunities either in the modern sector or in useful public works at constant—or slowly increasing—wage rates and to improve productivity (and hence *per capita* real income) in the backward traditional agricultural sector, rather than by rapidly increasing wage rates for those already in employment in the modern sector. To the extent that a kind of 'wages fund' mechanism operates in the short run, the aggregate size of the wages bill may be the same in both cases. The essential difference between them lies in the *composition of demand*; for in this kind of economy it is more than likely that a higher *per capita* wage level would be associated with a higher import-content in expenditure.

There are four further considerations. First, the 'supply price' of labour in the low-productivity traditional sectors of the economy may be increased because the relatively high wage rates paid by the modern sector may raise people's expectations as to what is a satisfactory return for their labour. The result of these high expectations may well be a reluctance to engage in low-productivity occupations, such as traditional agriculture, services, and handicrafts; and there may also be a lag in the supply of domestic food production behind the growth in demand. Under these circumstances, the 'surplus labour' in the economy manifests itself in open unemployment rather than in disguised unemployment.

Second, just as in the case of a fully employed industrial economy, an increase in wage rates faster than the growth in productivity will lead to increased costs in the particular industry or industries concerned; and, given the fact that the industry is likely to be a price taker rather than a price leader

74

in export markets, production can become uneconomic. This will adversely affect the expansion of economic activity as well as the growth of employment.

Third, a rapid rate of wage increases in the public sector, which may often employ a very large percentage of the labour force in such economies, can unbalance the government's budget and reduce employment on public works projects. On the other hand, in a developed country which will have a stronger fiscal system and, therefore, a higher marginal tax ratio with respect to wage increases, such increases in wage rates would not be expected to lead to the same fiscal strain.

Finally, the difficulties of producing capital goods economically rule out in small economies any significant 'compensatory' benefits which mechanization might have in the large under-developed countries.

One can express the gist of the above analysis by saying that, while Keynesian income analysis provides a set of tools of great versatility and adaptability, the relative importance of the variables stressed by Keynes (consumption, investment, exports, savings, and imports) as well as the values of the parameters (the multiplier, elasticity of supply, and the marginal propensity to import) differ from country to country according to the stage of development attained as well as the size of the economy. Keynesian tools, therefore, have to be applied with very great care when we are dealing with economies other than developed industrial ones.

The refusal to recognize the harmful effects of a rapid rate of wage increases in a small open economy derives from using the wrong model. All economic theories are *valid*—provided that they are internally consistent. But an economic theory can be useful as a guide to policy only if it is *relevant* to a particular society. And for it to be relevant it must take into account the structure of the economy, the behaviour of individuals and of governments, and the institutions in force. Many of the theories setting out the relationship between economic variables apply only to developed industrial economies and can be misleading or even dangerous when applied to different types of economy. This is what makes it so important for economists from the underdeveloped countries to modify existing models or to develop new ones.

We should not therefore be surprised when an authoritative report dealing with employment objectives in underdeveloped countries in general argued very forcibly in favour of wage restraint in the modern sector in order to promote a high level of investment and to expand employment opportunities.[36] The report, it should be noted, was written by a group of distinguished economists from Communist, Western, and underdeveloped countries. But for a rigorous model of the workings of a small open economy we are indebted to Dudley Seers,[37] who shows that in an open petroleum economy the expansion of employment will be faster, the more slowly wage rates increase as compared with exports, the lower are profit margins in respect of production for the home market, the higher are tax rates on companies producing exports, and the lower is the share of imports in domestic expenditure. He further shows that the most strategic relationship for employment is the first —the rate of increase of wages compared with the rate of increase of exports. Although I have reservations about its appropriateness as a long-run model, I think it provides a very relevant analysis of the workings of this type of economy in the short period.

In fact, in small open economies wage rates, employment, foreign exchange, and commercial policy are all intimately related one to another. In this sort of economy, where there is structural unemployment, the employment problem can be formulated in terms of the redistribution of supplies of foreign exchange for the purchase of imported wage goods from the employed to the unemployed. The employed can, through the wages they earn, command part of the supply of foreign exchange made available by exports for the purchase of imported

---

[36] I.L.O., Report of a Panel of Experts, *Employment Objectives in Economic Development*, Geneva, 1961, pp. 56–8. W. A. Lewis also shows how a high level of real wages in the West Indies is inimical to the expansion of employment. See his 'Employment Policy in an Under-Developed Area', *Social and Economic Studies*, September 1958.

[37] Seers, 'The Mechanism of an Open Petroleum Economy'.

wage goods; but the unemployed have no such access to the pool. Now, analytically speaking, foreign exchange for the purchase of wage goods can be redistributed from the employed to the unemployed by any of the following six methods: by a change in the exchange rate; by a halt in the increase of wage rates; by the taxation of companies producing exports; by taxation of the employed; by the employed shifting either voluntarily or through fiscal or commercial policy measures from spending on imports to spending on domestically produced goods; or by the adoption of the 'disequilibrium system', under which, domestic demand being made to expand faster than exports, the supply of foreign exchange (and therefore real wages) has to be rationed out between the previously employed and the newly employed. In practice, of course, these various methods are not mutually exclusive and appropriate combinations of them can be tried. And in practice, too, many of these methods may have to be deliberately avoided because of their probably adverse effects on other policy objectives, such as that of securing an inflow of private capital.

I should like to make it clear, however, that any argument in favour of restraint in wage increases in this type of economy must rest on the assumption that the income forgone by wage earners by not pressing for wage increases will be saved *and invested productively within the national economy.* This is an assumption which may not always hold and, to the extent that it does not, the argument must be qualified. Moreover, in enclave economies, where there is a large foreign-owned sector, the matter is further complicated by the consideration that increases in wage incomes in this sector add to the *national* income (defined as the income accruing to the residents of the country as against the income produced in the geographical area—the Gross Domestic Product), if the alternative to paying higher wages is for the companies to increase their payment of dividends abroad.[38] But it can be argued that the important objective is to use the wages forgone for *investment within the*

[38] On these assumptions the National Income is increased even though the increases in wages paid will be at the expense of government tax revenues paid by the companies.

country. To ensure this will almost certainly require the development of machinery for some kind of incomes policy. But this is easier said than done. Yet, unless it is done, the employment situation in such countries will probably get worse.

The problem of wage differentials in underdeveloped countries deserves some comment at this stage, although it cuts across the distinction between large closed and small open economies and although it raises wider issues than those of employment.

In underdeveloped countries certain classes of semi-skilled, skilled, or professional workers may be in short supply but their remuneration and prospects may compare unfavourably with those of, say, clerical and administrative grades, who may be in much ampler supply relatively to their demand. Furthermore, the situation is not likely to be static, since the relative supply-demand situation in respect of particular skills is often changing; and this implies that, in the interests of development, relative rates of remuneration ought to be changing as well. But such a periodical adjustment of the wage structure is difficult to effect, since existing differentials become hallowed with time and vested interests get built up.

Several issues are raised by an inappropriate structure of wages and salaries in an underdeveloped country. First, incentives will be lacking for people to undergo training in fields which are not properly remunerated. Moreover, much of the expenditure on the training institutions will be wasted. Second, the almost inevitable drift from the rural to the urban areas will be accelerated, aggravating the problems of open unemployment, housing, and social services and possibly reducing the food supply. Third, there could develop social discontent over the privileges enjoyed by the groups favoured by the wages—and salary—structure. Africa faces these problems in a most acute form, especially the third, because in colonial days clerical and administrative jobs were performed by expatriates who received very high levels of remuneration even in relation to similar jobs in their country of origin, and the heirs to the colonial rulers now demand the same privileges. But the

78

Caribbean is not exempt from these problems and here the situation is further aggravated by the modern enclave sector of the economy being able to pay relatively high wages. Why should, say, a truck driver employed in the oil industry get more pay than his counterpart with a similar level of skill, experience, and responsibility who happens to be employed by a small transport contractor? Why should an agricultural worker employed in the citrus industry receive less than one-half of the wage paid to unskilled workers who happen to be employed on public works? Or—to pose the question with regard to the relative rate of remuneration of skills within the same industry—why should a semi-skilled daily-paid worker receive more pay than his monthly-paid supervisor?

The problem is an extremely difficult one to solve in any non-totalitarian society. As is so often the case, diagnosis is much easier than the application of the remedy. But an effort clearly has to be made, if development is to proceed at the required rate. I am sometimes inclined to the view that, if the consent of the various social groups to an incomes policy is not forthcoming, the realization that illogical wage and salary structures are hindering development may well lead to the establishment of centralized control over incomes in both the public and private sectors in underdeveloped countries. And, once this happens, centralized control of all economic activity will inevitably follow.

There is, finally, yet another disadvantage of small size. Small countries *with good communications* suffer from the demonstration effect more actuely than larger ones where the population is more dispersed. In a small island of less than, say, 5,000 square miles where geographical obstacles do not impose great difficulties to the movement of persons and where communications are fairly well-developed, there is really no psychological distinction between town and country. For the countryman is in constant touch with the townsman and with life in the urban areas. He can see the high material standards attained by the better-off urban dweller and he can also see the collectively provided amenities available in the towns. The first reaction of course is not to improve his productivity to a level nearer that of industry but to wish to consume as much both privately and collectively as the better-off townsmen. Hence the propensity to consume, both privately and in the form of government services, goes up. In this situation the mobilization of small rural savings whether for agricultural co-operatives or for investment in government bonds becomes a matter of considerable difficulty.[39]

We have of course so far painted a tale of woe. This I have done deliberately in order to drive home the essential distinctions between a very large and a very small country. But there are certain compensations in smallness. I shall now outline what I consider to be the most important of these.

First of all, it may be held that it is important to be unimportant. A small country may be able to make certain gains which are not open to a large country. First, even if the demand for a particular commodity is income—or price—inelastic, the demand facing one particular small country may be rather highly *price*-elastic. This means that by making its price more competitive it may be able to capture more sales from other countries. Second, there is always the possibility of small countries developing exports of highly income-elastic specialty products for sale to a wide range of advanced countries. Although the sales to each country may be small in relation to the total import demand of the advanced countries, they may amount to a significant source of foreign exchange earnings for the small poor country.[40] Swiss watches and Scandinavian furniture are cases in point.

Third, a given volume of foreign resources (whether in the form of aid or private capital) can do much more for a small country than for a large one.

Fourth, a small country may be able to break the rules of the game by discrimination or otherwise and escape retaliation

[39] Professor Robert Mundell has pointed out to me that the demonstration effect could equally work the other way round and lead to an increase in productivity in the rural sector. The point is well taken, but it seems to me that the demonstration effect works more quickly in respect of consumption than of production.

[40] This possibility was suggested to me by Professor Kari Levitt.

simply because its import-demand is so small as to be negligible in the view of important exporters.

Fifth, a devaluation of the currency of a small country may not lead to a big deterioration in its commodity terms of trade *vis-à-vis* the rest of the world although, if it is to be effective in expanding export earnings and employment, it will entail a redistribution of real income between various groups *within* the country.

Yet it should be realized that these are advantages only if one country attempts to reap them. If a very large number of small countries attempted to realize such advantages, they would collectively no longer be unimportant and their actions would invite retaliation.

Sixth, small independent countries need not rely entirely on their own resources for defence, since they may find protection under the umbrella of collective security by negotiating defence pacts and military alliances.

Next, where there are good communications, the uniformity of tastes likely to be found in a small country whose people have a great deal of geographical mobility will mean that internal commodity markets will be unified and that they will be genuine *national* markets. And, of course, this will lead to the realization of economies of scale.

The last two advantages of small size relate to the fundamental social, political, and institutional parameters governing economic behaviour, whose importance I have been emphasizing throughout.

First, in a small country there is a presumption that national policies would be more easily and widely disseminated and therefore better understood. A very small country is a society of face-to-face contacts. In such a country it should therefore be possible for the goals and objectives as well as instruments and constraints of a national development plan—or, if there is no plan, of economic and social policies—to be widely understood. And it is obvious that a high degree of understanding at all levels of society is of great importance and effectiveness in democratic national planning.

Finally, we come to an advantage of smallness which has

been put forward by Kuznets.[41] Kuznets argues that a small nation is much more of a real community than a large nation in that there is a greater degree of social cohesion. Such a high degree of social cohesion is held to lead to two effects—one economic and the other social. The economic effect is to make the economy more resilient in the face of economic shocks of external origin. There does appear to be some support for this view if we look at already developed small economies such as Switzerland and Denmark. Consider for example the development of the co-operative movement and the switch from wheat to livestock products in Denmark in the 1870's and 1880's when the whole basis of the economy was threatened by the sharp fall in wheat prices as a result of American competition.

The social manifestation of the high degree of cohesiveness is the welfare state and a fairly equal distribution of income both between classes and geographical regions.

On the one hand, it is, to say the least, debatable whether in the small underdeveloped countries of today there is either a high degree of social cohesion or whether, if there is, it manifests itself in the ways envisaged by Kuznets. For one thing, the welfare state is often an ideological import stimulated by the operation of the international demonstration effect rather than a manifestation of a high degree of solidarity. On the other hand, I consider that a small community has the potential for developing a real democracy where there is a widespread popular participation and a strong sense of social cohesion.

Let us see where we have got so far. We have seen that the real constraint to economic growth in small overpopulated countries is the growth of the manufacturing sector on the basis of export markets, and that this is the most crippling disadvantage of small size.

It is time to return to the subject of exports of manufactures. A small country which has a high *per capita* income shows a high ratio of exports to G.D.P., and this is so whether or not transformation of the economy has been achieved. If transformation has not been achieved (the enclave economy case), the economy will be a heavy exporter of minerals, raw materials

[41] Kuznets, 'Economic Growth', pp. 27-30.

or other resource products experiencing favourable demand conditions in world markets. In the other case where transformation of the internal economy has been achieved, there will be a large ratio of exports to G.D.P. consisting either of primary and processed agricultural products (New Zealand and Denmark) or manufactured products (Switzerland, Belgium, and Hong Kong). Today many of the small underdeveloped countries cannot rely on a great expansion of exports of primary products because, as we have already indicated, demand conditions are often unfavourable. And they may wish to find employment for their surplus labour, if not directly in industry, at least through the repercussions of industrial expansion on employment offered by other economic sectors. Both situations point to the expansion of the manufacturing sector. Again, a small country earning a high income either from mineral or resource exports may experience either actual or potential diminishing returns and may wish to build up other sectors of the economy. This too points to the expansion of manufacturing production.

The older small manufacturing countries (Switzerland, Belgium, Holland, and Luxembourg) were able to develop manufacturing exports when there were fewer restrictions on world trade and fewer restrictive trading blocs and when the income-elasticity of demand for simple manufactured products was higher than it is today because world *per capita* incomes were lower then than they now are. Moreover, in those days economies of scale were less important since technological progress in a capital-intensive direction had not proceeded so far. This is the age of relatively large units of production. And, to the extent that the domestic market can be used as a point of departure for exports, the domestic market could suffice in those countries for the initial launching of the industrial development effort. These conditions of course do not apply to the contemporary world.

There are several reasons for this, the most prominent being restrictions against so-called 'cheap labour' imports into the markets of the industrial countries; wage rates in the underdeveloped countries which do not reflect the true cost of labour as determined by relative factor supplies; the low income-elasticity of demand in the advanced countries for the simpler, labour-intensive products; the fear of creating excess capacity in the face of the uncertainties of the world market; all the numerous factors inhibiting incursions into export markets; and, finally, the fact that nearly all underdeveloped countries are protecting the simpler labour-intensive final consumer goods.

Hong Kong has so far been a brilliant exception. Among the factors which made Hong Kong's breakthrough into world markets possible were low labour costs, a willingness to apply advanced technologies, and a readiness to shift from simple products such as textiles to some of the newer growth products, such as plastics and transistorized wireless sets. Even more important perhaps was the country's past history as an entrepôt trader as well as the complete absence of any alternative means of livelihood other than the export of manufactures.[42]

The difficulties of capturing exports of manufactured goods are formidable—although this is the appropriate strategy of development for such countries. It may be difficult for a small country to negotiate trade agreements for the sale of manufactures. In the face of these difficulties it is possible to advocate two alternative courses. One is near or full economic integration with a large country or large trading bloc—Puerto Rico *vis-à-vis* the U.S.A. and Luxembourg *vis-à-vis* the Benelux Union. The other is economic integration with neighbouring underdeveloped countries. The first alternative is open to objection on political grounds in that it may be held to be a form of 'neo-colonialism'. It should also be noted that, apart from the freeing of trade, additional positive policy instruments may have to be used to promote development in the less developed country. Integration in itself may do nothing to prevent the polarization between the more developed and the less developed parts of the Union.[43]

[42] U.N. Centre for Industrial Development, *Trade in Manufactures and Semi-Manufactures*, p. 104.

[43] Much has been written on this tendency towards polarization. The *locus classicus* is Gunnar Myrdal, *Economic Theory and Underdeveloped*

The second is the direction in which it appears more likely that many countries will move.

For my part, I am strongly convinced that small countries will increasingly tend to form economic groupings with each other of varying degrees of closeness—although I do not underestimate the enormous practical difficulties involved in this undertaking.[44] There has in fact been much discussion by the underdeveloped countries in recent years of projects of economic co-operation and economic integration. But only two have really taken shape—the Latin American Free Trade Area (L.A.F.T.A.) and the Central American Common Market.

This is not the place to deal fully with the economics of integration among small underdeveloped countries. But the subject is so central to the economic growth of such countries that I have to undertake a brief analysis of some of the major issues.

I shall start with the observation that the economic analysis of the benefits and disadvantages of economic integration between underdeveloped countries leaves much to be desired. This is so for two reasons. First, the analysis of customs unions is largely a branch of static welfare theory relying heavily on the neo-classical assumptions of full employment, perfect competition, constant returns to scale, perfect internal mobility of factors of production, the equality of private and social costs, etc.[45] The second is that the rationale of economic integration

---

Regions, London, 1957. See also Hirschman, The Strategy of Economic Development, pp. 183–201 and Belassa, The Theory of Economic Integration, Chapter 9. The Economics of Nationhood (Port-of-Spain), the Government of Trinidad and Tobago, 1959, also discusses this problem in relation to the former West Indies Federation.

[44] Apart from the obvious difficulties of getting various governments to work together, there is also the necessity of providing transport links which may entail heavy capital and recurrent expenditures. Without adequate regional transport facilities, the removal of trade barriers can often do nothing to promote integration.

[45] The two seminal theoretical contributions are J. Viner, The Customs Union Issue, New York, 1950, and J. Meade, The Theory of Customs Union, Amsterdam, 1955.

among underdeveloped countries is in many essential respects quite different from what it is among advanced ones.

A truly dynamic theory of economic integration is an essential part of any theory of development for small underdeveloped countries. But the neo-classical theory of integration has been of little use to such countries. Just as orthodox economics has failed the underdeveloped countries by presenting them with a static theory of comparative advantage, so has it failed them by offering them a similar theory of economic integration. Just as dynamic factors must be introduced into traditional international trade theory for it to be of any guidance to underdeveloped countries, so must there be developed a dynamic theory of economic integration applicable to small underdeveloped countries.

I became strikingly aware of this about four years ago when I was asked to write an article on the proposed West Indies Customs Union.[46] In that article I came to the conclusion that much of the analysis of customs-union problems applied to the advanced countries was not applicable to the West Indian case. In particular, I was not convinced of the alleged disadvantages of trade diversion as expounded by Viner.

Let me recall the neo-classical approach to the problem and indicate briefly its relevance to the problems of underdeveloped countries.

The theory envisages gains and losses for the participating countries, the Union as a whole and the outside world resulting from the following factors: the efficiency with which resources are used; and the effect on the terms of trade of the Union with the outside world.

But a moment's reflection reveals that this approach is both irrelevant and sterile when used to analyse the problem of integration among underdeveloped countries. The main con-

---

[46] W. G. Demas, 'The Economics of West Indies Customs Union', *Social and Economic Studies*, March 1960. See also the forthcoming paper by Alister McIntyre for a brilliant critique of the relevance of the neo-classical theory of economic integration to underdeveloped countries—*Decolonization and Trade Policy in the West Indies*, University of Puerto Rico.

cepts required in an analysis of the effects of integration among such countries are economies of scale, external economies, and polarization. The static allocation of resources through trade diversion and trade creation, effects on competition, and terms-of-trade effects are largely irrelevant, if not positively misleading. The neo-classical analysis pays attention only to economies of scale among these factors.[47]

In the neo-classical analysis under the first head of efficiency in resource use we have the famous production effects of trade creation and trade diversion and the more recondite consumption effects. We also have the effect of the Union in stimulating more competition between the partner countries. These are *par excellence* the neo-classical problems of resource allocation. However, I do not consider that the resource allocation benefit or loss is really very relevant to the situation of the countries which I have in mind.

Take the trade diversion argument. As is well known, trade diversion occurs when a partner country in the Union is forced to purchase from another member of the Union higher-cost imports which it formerly purchased at a lower cost from outside the Union. It is forced to switch to higher-cost sources of imports because internal free trade and the common external tariff allow the higher-cost source from within the Union to be more competitive. This is held to be bad for resource allocation.

But even in static terms the argument is not necessarily true for underdeveloped countries. For if there is unemployment or underemployment, the market wage rate will exceed the social opportunity-cost of labour and a protective tariff which compensates the entrepreneur for the divergence between the market price and the social cost of labour may be necessary to improve the allocation of resources from a purely static point of view. Once we admit the logical validity of the protectionist argument in a situation of imperfection in the labour market, we also have to admit that in certain circumstances trade

[47] Belassa's *Theory of Economic Integration* is one of the few academic studies to deal adequately with the dynamic aspects of economic integration.

diversion may not be a bad thing. This I argued four years ago; and I was therefore interested to see Dell make this his principal criticism of the neo-classical theory in his recent very realistic study on economic integration.[48] However, Dell presses the argument too far and ignores the fact that, although labour may be surplus and therefore free, the complementary capital is scarce and so has a positive social opportunity-cost.

Again, competition may not be so important as between the recently established existing industries of a group of under-developed countries. It does not make sense for a stronger infant to kill a weaker infant!

In dynamic terms, of course, the case for trade diversion in underdeveloped countries, especially in respect of increments of demand, is much stronger. It is precisely through such a diversion of increases in demand from imports from outside the area to future production by member countries that a customs union confers benefits on member countries. The widening of the market must occur in practice much more through diversion of incremental trade to countries within the integrated area rather than through trade creation in respect of existing trade. For it would be unrealistic to expect member countries of the integrated area to aquiesce in the disappearance of their new industries for the sake of an abstraction called 'economic integration'. As we saw in the first chapter, the creation of an economic region can mean that the development pattern for *the region as a whole* can approximate more to import-substitution—although from the point of view of individual member countries there will still be a large volume of 'exports' to and 'imports' from other member countries.

It is important to note however that integration may often not remove the necessity to seek export markets outside the region. The Union may merely assist in building up an industrial structure which must still be largely geared to outside markets. And in fact the two processes—greater trade within the region and exports to the outside world—will have to take place concurrently. This may not necessarily be undesirable when we recall the difficulties (referred to above) experienced

[48] Dell, pp. 212–14.

88

by countries with inward-looking patterns of industrial development when they seek to become major exporters.

On the terms-of-trade argument, all that I will say is that it has more force in a customs union among the great economic powers with large exporting and importing capacity relatively to the rest of the world than among a group of small and relatively weak countries.

I come now to what I consider to be the most important mechanism by which integration confers benefits on underdeveloped countries—the stimulus to new investment arising from the prospects of achieving economies of scale and external economies. Some economists looking at the E.E.C. are sceptical whether the economies-of-scale argument carries much weight in this particular case. This is because the European national economies seem already to be enjoying all the benefits of economies of scale that are open to them and consequently the removal of tariff barriers between them will not make much difference. But, as we have seen, in the small underdeveloped countries, the situation is just the opposite. Here the possibility of capturing economies of scale and externalities constitutes the real justification for economic integration. It is also possible that economic integration could lead to a unified and possibly broader capital market in the region and so assist in mobilizing resources. Provided that the integrated area is large enough, balanced growth in supply and in demand can also come to have some meaning and relevance to small countries.

Last, but not least, it has to be stressed that divergent rates of growth as between different parts of the economically integrated area are overwhelmingly probable. The reason for such divergence lies in the well-known polarization effects of growth, especially in the modern sector of the economy. Polarization can be explained in terms of the external economies generated by poles of growth in one geographical area of a country or in one country of an integrated region. It is particularly likely to occur in a customs union between underdeveloped countries where one country has started its industrial development earlier or between an advanced country and an underdeveloped one. Under such circumstances, even if integration leads to a maxi-

89

mization of the rate of growth of the *area as a whole*, this will be little comfort to those countries which either lag behind (or conceivably retrogress) in manufacturing industry.

Short of political union between the countries either through a federation or a unitary state leading almost automatically to a transfer of income from richer to poorer units through the operations of the fiscal system, economic integration has to be accompanied by positive measures, if it is to be acceptable to the poorer members. One such type of measure is the one which takes place automatically in a single political unit—a transfer of income through the fiscal system. Another type would aim at ensuring that by conscious governmental (or preferably inter-governmental) action, growth points of modern manufacturing are created in each country or in a large enough number of countries. A third type of positive measure would be for a country with an advantage in manufacturing to agree to withdraw, or refrain from increasing, resources devoted to production of an agricultural commodity which a less advanced country is capable of producing in increasing amounts.[49]

And then there are the practical considerations such as the need to adjust to loss of revenue consequent upon the removal of tariffs between the members of the Union, the need to spend possibly large sums on developing regional transport facilities, and the need to start with limited rather than complete forms of integration.

The recognition of the necessity to prevent polarization through positive government intervention and the possible desirability on practical grounds of beginning with attenuated forms of integration might well lead to certain arrangements which would be anathema to the orthodox and would almost certainly violate the rules of the game as now formulated.

Let us attempt to summarize by pulling together the various strands of the argument:

1. Small countries, like large ones, have to transform their economies if they want development.

2. In a very large country transformation of the economy can possibly produce self-sustained growth, but in a very small

[49] See McIntyre, *Decolonization and Trade Policy.*

country the degree of self-sustenance of the growth process is less because of greater external dependence. Most countries of course fall in between these extreme cases.

3. In a continental economy transformation involves a balanced pattern of development with exports and imports playing a marginal, balancing role. There may however be acute balance-of-payments problems during the takeoff of such economies.

4. In a very small economy there are limits to import-substitution, and transformation usually involves the export of manufactured goods unless (a) the country has primary or resource exports in high demand, or (b) there is not heavy population pressure in agriculture.

5. A small country which has to produce manufactures finds this difficult for a number of reasons, the most crucial being the existence of economies of scale in the production of most kinds of manufactured goods.

6. This implies an export drive coupled with, where possible, varying forms of economic co-operation between such countries.

7. A dynamic theory of economic integration is an essential element in the economics of development of small countries. The neo-classical approach is inappropriate in this context and a new theoretical approach has to be worked out.

8. The Keynesian analysis has to be applied with great care to underdeveloped economies, all the more so to small open ones.

9. Apart from the smallness of the domestic market, there are other disadvantages in small size, the most important being the difficulty of preventing the export of savings and the sacrifice of domestic employment to balance-of-payments equilibrium in an open economy and the difficulty of developing a broadly based capital market.

10. Among the economic advantages of small size are 'the importance of being unimportant' in external commercial policy, more unified national markets, greater flexibility, and perhaps greater potential social cohesion.

PART II: APPLICATION TO THE CARIBBEAN

CHAPTER III: CHARACTERISTICS OF THE CARIBBEAN ECONOMIES

In this and the subsequent chapter I shall seek to apply the general framework set out in Part I to the specific case of the Caribbean.

In this chapter I shall outline very briefly what I conceive to be the principal characteristics and problems of the Caribbean economies and indicate also very briefly my reasons for believing that development is urgently required today in the area. The discussion of characteristics and problems does not seek to be exhaustive nor is there any attempt to present a thorough survey of the structure and recent history of these economies.[1] This is a task which in itself would require volumes. All I shall seek to do is to present the characteristics which are relevant to the general framework previously outlined and to the problems of planning discussed in the next chapter. In other words, the data I shall present here are meant to be purely illustrative and are by no means exhaustive.

The first problem is to define the term 'Caribbean'. Here I take the Caribbean to include the ten former members of the West Indies Federation: Jamaica, Trinidad and Tobago, Barbados, the four Windward Islands and the three Leeward Islands, and British Guiana. In other words, I am referring to what used to be called the British Caribbean and which, now that Jamaica and Trinidad and Tobago have become independent, is now called the Caribbean Commonwealth countries. It

[1] A very competent macro-economic study of the economic development of Trinidad and Tobago in the 1950's is to be found in Frank Rampersad's 'Growth and Structural Change in the Trinidad and Tobago Economy 1951–1961', Central Statistical Office, Research Papers No. 1 (Port-of-Spain), December 1963.

should be noted, however, that in terms of regional integration the Caribbean might have to assume a wider meaning and include the Dutch and French mainland and island territories, Puerto Rico, and the independent republics. The broader definition would give the region a total population of 21·8 million as against a population of 3·8 million in the narrower definition.

As Table I indicates, individual units of the Caribbean Commonwealth countries are very tiny economies and the area as a whole, even if economically integrated, would still be a very small economy. Even so, I think a useful distinction can be made between the 'larger' territories of Jamaica, Trinidad and Tobago, British Guiana, and perhaps Barbados, on the one hand and the 'smaller' territories of the Leeward and Windward Islands on the other hand. It should not be forgotten that the Leewards and Windwards are separate islands, most of them having between 70,000 and 90,000 inhabitants: Montserrat, the smallest, having 13,000. Moreover, British Guiana is in many respects a small island since, in spite of its total area of 83,000 square miles, only a narrow coastal strip is inhabited. Finally, the high population densities and high rates of natural increase should be observed.

While I shall include the Leeward and Windward Islands in the description which follows, what I have to say about planning in the next chapter will relate principally to the 'bigger' countries of Jamaica, Trinidad and Tobago, British Guiana, and Barbados.

The Leeward and Windward Islands are so small as to fall into a separate category and, while this factor in itself does not preclude the development of manufacturing industry, it appears to me that their future is much more closely bound up with exports of traditional primary products, the growth in productivity of the domestic food-producing sector and the development of the tourist industry. Moreover, the economies of the 'larger' territories are capable of sustaining more sophisticated financial institutions.

The Caribbean, by reason of its long historical association with the Western world and its close proximity to the North American continent, has been overcome—perhaps more than

TABLE I

CARIBBEAN POPULATION DATA

	Population 1961	Area Square Miles	Density per Square Mile	Natural Rate* of Increase during 1960 %
Jamaica	1,630,000	4,411	370	3·3
Trinidad and Tobago	859,000	1,980	418	3·1
British Guiana	580,000	83,000	7	3·3
Barbados	235,000	166	1,395	2·5
Leewards and Windwards	437,600 (1960)	1,182	370	3·2

* Excludes emigration and immigration.

SOURCE: 'Estimates of Inter-Censal Population by Age and Sex and Revised Vital Rates for British Caribbean Countries 1946–1960', Census Research Programme Publication (Port-of-Spain), 1964, and official government publications.

most other areas—by the revolution of rising expectations. In consequence of this and as a result of the impact of advertising through the news media, consumption functions have been pushed upwards. There is a widespread desire for many of the more expensive durable consumer goods associated with North American civilization, and consumer credit (or hire-purchase) facilities are increasingly providing the means to satisfy this desire. In addition, increasing demands are being made for the provision of expanded and improved governmental welfare services.

In considering the development of the Caribbean economies we have to bear in mind two fundamental institutional constraints: the existence of political democracy on classic Westminster lines and the existence of a strong independent and forceful trade-union movement sharing the philosophy of North American, and to a lesser degree, British trade unionism. These constraints are not of course unique to the Caribbean—although I suspect that in few other underdeveloped countries is the trade-union movement so imbued with ideas and attitudes more appropriate to the advanced countries. This stems not only from the commendable, though often misplaced, idealism of certain international organizations but from the close proximity to North America and the general 'openness' of the society which makes for very close contacts with the trade-union movements in Britain and North America.

The consequences of these social and institutional parameters for the development process are not difficult to discern. First, the existence of political democracy and the possibility of alternative governments can bring to the forefront the quite justifiable demands of the population for immediate and badly needed improvements, especially in social services; and since resources are always limited, this can conflict with long-run objectives of promoting structural changes in the economy. Second, the trade unions can and often do pursue policies which secure short-term gains in real wages and working conditions for their membership at the expense of the expansion of employment opportunities, capital formation, and the government budget.

˙Even a nodding acquaintance with the historical development process of the advanced countries—the U.K., Japan, and the U.S.S.R., to take only three extreme types—suggests that full-blown political democracy and a free unfettered trade-union movement can impose severe constraints on the growth process. For historically these institutions are to be viewed as the *products* rather than the *concomitants* of the developed process. To recognize this is not of course to deny the intrinsic value of these two institutions. Even though the economist may accept such intrinsic values, he is professionally bound to draw attention to the wide area of incompatibility between them and the desire for rapid economic development. The point that is being made here is that the preservation of parliamentary democracy and an independent trade-union movement is conditional upon an even greater development effort than would otherwise be necessary.

I have emphasized some of the negative features of the institutions of parliamentary democracy and free trade unionism. Yet it would be wrong to ignore the positive aspects.

In an underdeveloped country trade unions can play a positive role in giving dignity to the wage relationship; in promoting increased productivity; in inculcating discipline, in providing welfare facilities, and in encouraging and mobilizing savings from their membership. Most important in the Caribbean, the trade unions in the modern sector of the economy can do much for employment by pursuing wage policies which are appropriate to Caribbean conditions rather than those copied from the wholly different situation of advanced countries.

Generally speaking, it is remarkable how little thought has been given either in the advanced or the underdeveloped countries to the role of the trade-union movement in a nationalist ex-colonial society aiming at rapid economic development. In a totalitarian one-party state the problem does not arise, since the interests of associations such as trade unions are made to coincide with those of the state and of the society. In fact, in such a country all associations are appendages of the state. But in a pluralistic society the dilemma has to be squarely faced and possible solutions devised.

99

From a nationalist standpoint, trade unions have undoubt-edly been a progressive force in Caribbean society. The move-ment has been from its inception intimately associated with, and often in the vanguard of, the struggle for political indepen-dence. It has also been responsible for removing the grosser forms of exploitation by foreign capital which existed even up to the 1950's. But it is clear that, now that the case of political nationalism has been won in Jamaica, and Trinidad and Tobago and is on the verge of being won in the other territories and now that important economic concessions have been won from foreign capital, the unions have a somewhat different role to play in future.

It is too easy to say that the unions are to blame for not having perceived their new role. The problem goes very deep and involves the whole community. For a new role can be devised for the unions only as part of the wider task facing Caribbean society of evolving economic and social arrange-ments which provide for the needs of the rural population, the unorganized urban workers and the unemployed as well as those of organized labour, while at the same time ensuring that the income produced by foreign capital is equitably divided between the companies on the one hand and the people and government of the community on the other hand. One of the effects of the dual economic structure of the Caribbean has been to create an aristocracy of organized labour in the modern sector. The gap between organized labour on the one hand and the rest of the labour force has two consequences. The first is that it tends to increase the amount of migration to the urban areas, the consequences of which are obvious. The second aspect of the gap is more social than economic. It unfairly stratifies the population of working age into the privileged and the underprivileged under circumstances unrelated to any rational criteria.

I have also said that full-blown parliamentary democracy has a negative influence on development in so far as demands for immediate improvements do not sufficiently take into ac-count the economic resources of the country. This negative influence is enhanced in countries experiencing a rapid growth of population. There is therefore the important task for political leaders and social scientists in the Caribbean of determining how far plans should go in meeting popular demands without compromising the basic objectives of long-run improvement.

The positive side of democracy in economic planning is that it can provide the opportunities for the participation of the people in the development process. But the exploitation of such opportunities is not automatic. It depends on political leadership and on the development of appropriate mechanisms to make such participation a reality.

It is a fact that *per capita* incomes, especially in Trinidad and Tobago and Jamaica, are higher than in many underdeveloped countries; further, both these countries experienced high annual growth rates in the Gross Domestic Product of the order of 8 per cent per annum throughout the nineteen-fifties.

Neither of these facts necessarily reflects the achievement of an advanced stage of structural transformation. The large divergence between the Gross Domestic Product on the one hand and the Gross National Product and the National Income on the other hand, as revealed in Table II, is a reminder of continued heavy foreign investment in the enclave export industries without which the high growth rates could never have been recorded.

The relatively high *per capita* income of the smaller territories as compared with many of the economies of Africa and South-East Asia is probably due to a greater degree of specialization, reflecting the greater pervasiveness of the money as opposed to the subsistence economy and also perhaps a longer period of participation in international trade. The fast rates of growth of *per capita* real product, real income, and real consumption in Trinidad and Tobago and Jamaica are in part deceptive in that they were the reflection of fortuitous circumstances which are hardly likely to recur—such as the rapid expansion of the mineral-exporting sectors—oil in Trinidad and Tobago and bauxite in Jamaica. In Jamaica, there was in addition the emigration outlet for surplus labour in the U.K. In fact favourable fortuitous circumstances operated in all the territories. Apart from the existence of emigration outlets, there was the

TABLE II

G.D.P., G.N.P., AND NATIONAL INCOME (WEST INDIAN DOLLARS)

		G.D.P. at Factor Cost per capita	G.N.P. at Factor Cost per capita	National Income per capita
Jamaica[1]	(1962)	734	706	658
Trinidad and Tobago[2]	(1962)	1180	1058	920
British Guiana[3]	(1960)	469	450	414
Barbados[4]	(1961)	502	n.a.	n.a.
Leewards and Windwards[4]	(1961)	337	n.a.	n.a.

SOURCES

[1] Jamaica, *Five-Year Independence Plan 1963–1968* and *Economic Survey 1963*.

[2] *Trinidad and Tobago, Draft Second Five-Year Plan 1964–1968*.

[3] A. Kundu, 'Inter-Industry Table for British Guiana 1959 and National Accounts 1957–1960', *Social and Economic Studies*, Supplement to Vol. XII, No. 1.

[4] C. O'Loughlin, *Survey of Economic Potential and Capital Needs of Barbados and the Windward and Leeward Islands*, London: H.M.S.O., 1963.

guaranteeing of sugar markets in the U.K. under the Commonwealth Sugar Agreement, the development of the tourist industry, and the development of the banana industry in the
Windward Islands. Many of these favourable factors are un-
likely to operate with the same force in the 1960's, in particular
the availability of emigration outlets and the rapid growth of
production of bauxite in Jamaica and of oil in Trinidad and
Tobago. Even the Commonwealth Preference system is in
question.

Within their limited resources, the governments of the territories have done as much as they could for education, health,
and the other public services. Compared with many other poor
countries, social services have attained a fairly high standard in
the Caribbean, although availability still lags woefully behind
the levels demanded by the population and their quality is
often deficient.

This is not the place to attempt an inventory of the physical
and natural resources. Suffice it to say that in each territory the
range of resources is highly skewed. For the area as a whole the
only major natural resources, apart from agricultural land and
tourist attractions, are petroleum and natural gas in Trinidad
and bauxite in Jamaica and British Guiana. Coal and iron ore
are generally speaking non-existent. The resource potential of
British Guiana—apart from bauxite—is still largely an un-
known quantity.

Thus we have a correspondingly skewed type of export trade,
heavily dependent on two basic resources: bauxite and alumina
plus sugar and sugar products account for 76 per cent of
Jamaican domestic exports, while petroleum, sugar and sugar
products account for 90 per cent of Trinidad and Tobago
domestic exports.

Further, earnings from exports constitute a very high proportion of national income. All of this is to be seen in Table III,
which shows characteristics of the area's foreign trade.

If tourist income were added, the dependence on external
sources of income would be even greater, especially in Jamaica,
Barbados, and the Leewards and Windwards.

We may also note the low share of manufactures in total

103

TABLE III

CHARACTERISTICS OF FOREIGN TRADE

A. EXPORTS

	Year	Ratio of Exports to G.D.P. %	Ratio of Imports to G.D.P. %
Jamaica[1]	1961	24·8	30·9
Trinidad and Tobago[2]	1961	59·3 (1962)	64·5 (1961)
British Guiana[3]	1960	50·0	55·5
Barbados[4]	1961	32·0	68·8
Leewards and Windwards[4]	1961	27·0	59·3

B. IMPORTS

SELECTED COMMODITY GROUPS AS A PERCENTAGE OF TOTAL IMPORTS

	Jamaica[1] %	Trinidad and Tobago[5] %	British Guiana[6] %
Food, Drink, and Tobacco	21·2	13·8	18·7
Raw Materials	21·5	51·8	18·6
Manufactured Goods	34·7	20·6	32·7

1 *Jamaica Independence Plan 1963–1968*.
2 *Trinidad and Tobago Five-Year Plan 1964–1968*.
3 Kundu, 'Inter-Industry Table for British Guiana'.
4 O'Loughlin, *A Survey of Economic Potential and Capital Needs*.
5 Rampersad, 'Growth and Structural Change in Trinidad and Tobago'.
6 Calculated from official government reports.

104

exports. If we exclude the processing of primary export staples (e.g. alumina, sugar, rum and molasses, and petroleum products) we find that exports of manufactures are practically non-existent, except in Jamaica where they amounted to 6·9 per cent of total exports in 1962.

Another aspect of the dependence on petroleum, bauxite, and sugar is the high rate of domestic capital formation, heavily financed by foreign resources. (If we were to include depreciation allocations, the share of foreign resources would be even greater.) We may note the complementary, low share of the public sector in total capital formation (Table IV).

The importance of mining and processing of minerals in Jamaica, British Guiana, and Trinidad and Tobago again emerges from an examination of the industrial origin of G.D.P. as shown in Table V. In the case of Trinidad and Tobago the mineral sector dominates the economy, accounting for 30 per cent of G.D.P. Manufacturing, including the processing of agricultural crops, but excluding the processing of minerals, has attained fairly respectable levels in Trinidad and Tobago (12·6 per cent of G.D.P.) and in Jamaica (13 per cent of G.D.P.), but contributes little or nothing in the smaller islands and in British Guiana. This sector includes a limited amount of intermediate and capital goods such as building materials and paints, but the bulk of the output consists of consumer goods in both Jamaica and Trinidad and Tobago. The importance of agriculture in the smaller islands is apparent.

It is important to note that the low share of agriculture in Trinidad and Tobago and in Jamaica does not represent an advanced degree of transformation. Rather, in both islands it is simply a reflection of the profound *malaise* of food production for the home market. In Trinidad and Tobago between 1951 and 1961 the rate of growth of this sector (excluding poultry and livestock) was slower than the rate of population increase, while in Jamaica it probably stagnated.

In fact, there is sharp dualism within the agricultural sector of most Caribbean countries. On the one hand, there is the estate or plantation producing crops usually geared to the export market and using relatively large amounts of capital per

TABLE IV

CAPITAL FORMATION IN THE CARIBBEAN

	Gross Domestic Capital Formation $ millions (W.I.)	Share of Domestic Capital Formation in G.D.P.	Share of Foreign Capital Inflow* In Total Capital Formation	Share of Public Sector in Total Capital Formation
	%	%	%	%
Jamaica (1960)[1]	248·6	23·3	30·9	10·0
Trinidad and Tobago (1962)[2]	298·3	29·8	33·6	21·6
British Guiana (1960)[3]	85·4	28·6	34·6	n.a.
Barbados (1961)[4]	32·1	13·8	49·0	n.a.

* Balance of payments deficit on current account, which includes *all* net accruals of foreign profits even where they may be reinvested in the country.

SOURCES

[1] *Jamaica Independence Plan 1963–1968.*
[2] *Trinidad and Tobago Five-Year Plan 1964–1968.*
[3] Kundu, 'Inter-Industry Table for British Guiana'.
[4] O'Loughlin. *A Survey of Economic Potential and Capital Needs.*

106

man and relatively advanced techniques. On the other hand, there is the peasant who produces either export staples or food for the home market or, as is common, both at the same time. Here capital per head is smaller and the techniques employed less advanced than in plantation agriculture and this fact reflects itself in lower yields per man and lower yields per acre in peasant agriculture.

The export sector, although more efficient, is also vulnerable. In the case of several crops—bananas in the Windwards, sugar in Jamaica, Trinidad and Tobago, Barbados, British Guiana, and the Leewards, citrus in Jamaica, and Trinidad and Tobago —remunerative production is vitally dependent on special preferences or special commodity agreements granted principally by the U.K. and to a smaller extent by Canada. These preferences are important because the Caribbean countries are high-cost producers of these commodities.

Dualism within the agricultural sector is only a manifestation of the more general phenomenon of dualism in the Caribbean economy. Thus a comparison of employment by industrial sector with output by industrial sector reveals striking contrasts in output per man: in Trinidad and Tobago, for instance, average output per man was $22,393 in petroleum mining and processing, some eight-and-a-half times as high as average output in manufacturing—$2,585 or in agriculture—$2,040. Employment by sectors is shown in Table VI.

Incidentally, we must note that the relatively low percentage of employment in agriculture in Trinidad and Tobago (21 per cent) should not be taken as an index of transformation. Like the small share of output, it is a sign of *malaise*, and it represents both the dominance of oil and the neglect of agricultural production for domestic consumption.

Third, the important share of the tertiary or service sectors does not only reflect transformation but also the large volume of underemployment and lack of opportunities for more productive employment.

The unemployment picture is somewhat confused because of the conceptual and definitional problems of measuring unemployment and underemployment. In particular, two sets of

TABLE V

INDUSTRIAL ORIGIN OF GROSS DOMESTIC PRODUCT (PERCENTAGES)

	1961 Jamaica[1]	1961 Trinidad and Tobago[2]	1960 British Guiana[3]	1956 Barbados[4]	1961 Leewards and Windwards[5]
Agriculture, Forestries, and Fisheries	12·7	11·8	27·2	33·7	38·6
Mining and Processing	8·6	30·8	8·6	0·6	} 1·9
Manufacturing	13·3	12·6	10·2	17·4	9·6
Construction	11·2	5·0	11·2	7·6	17·7
Government	7·9	9·8	9·8	10·0	included in manufacturing
Public Utilities	1·1	3·5	0·9		
Transport and Communications	6·9	3·8	7·0	6·3	2·2
Distribution	15·8	12·8	14·6	10·8	14·7
All Other Sources	22·5	9·9	10·4	13·6	15·3

SOURCES

1 *Economic Survey*, Jamaica, 1962.
2 Rampersad, 'Growth and Structural Change in Trinidad and Tobago'.
3 Kundu, 'Inter-Industry Table for British Guiana'.
4 J. Bethel, 'A National Accounts Study of the Economy of Barbados', *Social and Economic Studies*, IX, No. 2, June 1960.
5 O'Loughlin, *A Survey of Economic Potential and Capital Needs*.

estimates are available, based on different definitions. The definition which we use here is 'those persons of working age, able to work, wanting and having actively sought work within one month prior to the survey'. On this basis unemployment in 1960 amounted to 12·7 per cent, 10·6 per cent, and 11·3 per cent of the respective labour forces in Jamaica, Trinidad and Tobago, and British Guiana. Underemployment is also very severe; in the absence of generally agreed definitions and procedures for measurement we do not give any data. Suffice it to say that underemployment is severe whether measured in terms of numbers of the labour force engaged in low-productivity and low-income occupations or in terms of man-months worked.[2]

One of the most remarkable phenomena of contemporary social science is that total output can grow quite rapidly without a corresponding, or indeed significant, increase in employment. Many of the Caribbean economies have exhibited this phenomenon in greater or lesser degree. For example, in Puerto Rico, while very rapid rates of growth of output have been experienced since the institution of the 'Fomento' programme in the forties, unemployment has remained at a very high level of some 13 to 14 per cent of the labour force. Other countries, too, outside the Caribbean have undergone similar experiences: in India the absolute amount of unemployment actually increased over the period of the second Five-Year Plan in spite of the notable progress achieved in total output as well as in infrastructure and other fields.

The genesis of the employment problem in the Caribbean is the high rate of growth of the labour force (currently 2·4 per cent per annum in Trinidad and Tobago) combined with the capital-intensive nature of modern technology. This is the simple but fundamental explanation and is of course not peculiar to the Caribbean. Not only have capital-intensive processes characterized many of the new industries, but labour-saving devices have been introduced into major existing indus-

[2] A good analysis of the employment situation in Trinidad and Tobago for the period 1946 to 1960 is given in Jack Harewood, 'Employment in Trinidad and Tobago', *C.S.O. Research Papers*, No. 1, December 1963 (Port-of-Spain).

Table VI

EMPLOYMENT BY SECTORS 1960 (PERCENTAGES)

	Jamaica	Trinidad and Tobago	British Guiana	Barbados	Leewards and Windwards
Agriculture	39·0	21·1	37·0	26·4	46·0
Mining and Quarrying	0·7	4·9	3·8	0·6	0·2
Manufacturing*	14·8	15·5	16·3	15·2	11·2
Construction	8·2	11·4	8·0	10·5	10·8
Transport and Communications	3·2	6·2	4·8 —	5·2	3·7
Distribution	9·9	13·3	11·3	17·3	9·7
Other Services	24·2	27·5	18·8	24·7	18·3
Total	100·0	100·0	100·0	100·0	100·0

* Includes processing of mineral and agricultural products, except in British Guiana, where alumina processing is included under 'Mining'.

SOURCES: 1960 Census Data; and J. Harewood, 'Employment in Trinidad and Tobago', Central Statistical Office, Research Papers, No. 1 (Port-of-Spain), December 1963.

tries—especially petroleum and sugar, where employment has actually declined in recent years.

However, as we have seen, the employment problem in the Caribbean has been further aggravated by recent wage tendencies which have had three effects.

The first is one we have already referred to: the understandable urge by trade unions to extend to other less productive sectors the wage levels obtaining in the highly productive sectors, which then have neither the incentive nor the means to create jobs. The relatively high wage rates obtainable in the modern sector also convert underemployment or low-productivity employment into open unemployment by raising the 'supply price' of labour. This occurs because the expectations of what constitutes a 'reasonable' income are raised and, short of receiving this 'reasonable' income, individuals prefer to remain unemployed rather than engage in low-productivity occupations such as peasant agriculture, services, or handicrafts.

This effect is quite distinct from the influence that a rapid rate of increase in wage rates in a particular industry may have on the substitution of machines (always imported in the Caribbean) for local labour. This argument, although often put forward dogmatically, should not always be uncritically accepted. Its validity depends on the ratio of wage costs to other costs in the particular industry concerned and on the extent to which the product it makes has to face competition abroad. The truth of the matter may well be that in many modern industries more mechanized techniques are simply more efficient than less mechanized ones, even where wage rates are relatively low. To recognize this, however, is not to deny that big increases in wage rates or the desire to minimize the numbers employed in conditions of unsettled labour relations may *accelerate* the introduction of more mechanized techniques.

The third effect has also been analysed already. It is based on the Seers model of the functioning of an open petroleum economy in the short period when an increase in wage rates which is faster than the rate of increase in exports may, through the operation of a sort of 'wages-fund' mechanism, check the expansion of employment.

Many—in fact nearly all—underdeveloped countries have 'surplus labour'. But what makes the situation in the Caribbean so explosive potentially is the large amount of open unemployment in the towns, especially among young people. On the other hand, in less urbanized countries, surplus labour which takes the form of disguised unemployment in the rural areas may perhaps be tolerated by its victims for a longer period.

It has often been pointed out—quite correctly—that there has been real progress in the employment situation in the Caribbean in that the jobs created in modern industry have been well-paid high-productivity jobs, even though these have been inadequate in number and often at the expense of existing lower-productivity jobs (as in Puerto Rico). It is clear, however, that from a social point of view, such a state of affairs cannot entirely be regarded with equanimity by policy-makers.

The public finance system in the Caribbean has three features worth mentioning.

The first is the pressure on governmental capital and recurrent expenditures exerted by the rapid rate of growth of population. This pressure is felt particularly in the field of education. The consequence of the decline in death rates in recent years is the large number of children of school age; and this group is growing even faster than the general population. In Trinidad and Tobago the percentage of the population aged fifteen years and under is as high as 42 per cent.

Second, there is no capital market in any of the countries and this restricts the ability of governments to borrow large amounts locally for the financing of capital expenditures.

Third, incentives in the form of income-tax holidays and other fiscal concessions are granted to the growing sectors of the economy, in particular manufacturing, tourism, and petroleum. This means that the increase in revenue tends to lag behind the growth of the Gross Domestic Product; and this of course adversely affects the recurrent balance of the government's budget. It also means that personal incomes and personal expenditures bear a disproportionate share of the burden of fiscal imposts as compared with company income.

The result of these three features is heavy reliance on foreign aid in spite of very commendable fiscal efforts by the governments.

Except in Jamaica, which has a central bank, the monetary system of the Caribbean is the characteristic colonial Currency Board system. In its pure form, this system, which in essence is a very rigid form of the Gold Standard, requires 100 per cent backing in the form of sterling assets for local currency. Recently the system has been modified to allow for a small fiduciary issue. The Currency Board system implies that sterling and local currency are automatically convertible into one another at fixed rates of exchange in unlimited amounts. This in turn implies that Caribbean governments cannot impose exchange controls against the pound sterling. Further, the commercial banks are all branches of banks with head offices overseas. In theory this monetary system could work to ensure that the rate of growth of the money supply—and so of domestic expenditure—is rigidly tied to the state of the balance of payments (on both current and capital account); but the connection may not be so rigid because of 'autonomous' action by the commercial banks in extending credit locally independently of the state of the balance of payments.[3]

But even if the commercial banks bring in funds from outside to create local credit, independently of movements in the balance of payments, the local managers of the economy have no control over the monetary situation.

It should also be noted that the establishment of the Central Bank in Jamaica has not created an independent currency nor does the Bank possess any real possibility of monetary management of the economy.[4]

It should be emphasized that in this dependent monetary

[3] See Analyst, 'Currency and Banking in Jamaica', *Social and Economic Studies*, 1953 and C. Y. Thomas, 'The Balance of Payments and Money Supplies in a Colonial Economy', *Social and Economic Studies*, March 1963. The first is the pioneering and the second the definitive study of colonial monetary arrangements in the Caribbean.

[4] See Lloyd Best and Alister McIntyre, 'A First Appraisal of Monetary Management in Jamaica', *Social and Economic Studies*, September 1961.

system deficit financing is ruled out and consequently there is not much possibility of domestic inflation, the domestic price level being largely determined by movements in export and import prices. Thus Caribbean economic development has not been plagued with the monetary vicissitudes which have affected so many other developing countries.

Commercial and exchange control policies have been characterized by a high degree of openness. We have seen that there can be no exchange controls against sterling because the monetary system requires automatic convertibility between the local currency and sterling. When Britain moved to sterling convertibility in 1958, all the Caribbean Commonwealth countries followed automatically. Import licensing on the whole is not widely used to protect local industry, except in Jamaica which has recently acceded to the G.A.T.T. and which may therefore be expected not to intensify such controls. The tariff is in fact the main instrument of protection in the Caribbean. In 1962 Trinidad and Tobago modernized her tariff structure by increasing duties on durable consumer goods and on commodities being produced or capable of being produced locally and lowering duties on, or freeing, machinery and raw materials in order to protect local industry and assist the balance of payments. This was an important and historic step away from the colonial economic system; but by and large the Caribbean economies, including Trinidad and Tobago, still remain highly open in terms of commercial and foreign exchange policies.

It is interesting to observe one of the absurd aspects of the open economy in the Caribbean. This is the availability of consumer credit (or hire-purchase) facilities for the purchase of imported durable consumer goods. Hire-purchase booms have in more than one case been financed by an inflow of foreign capital! Not only does the system permit of external borrowing to finance consumption; such borrowing is used to finance imports of luxuries or semi-luxuries when there is a large amount of domestic unemployment and when the glaring necessity exists to mobilize domestic resources for development. Needless to say, advertising conspires with the existence of consumer credit facilities to lure people to the delights provided by the gadgets of modern civilization.

The extent of Caribbean economic co-operation is at present limited. Intraregional trade in 1962 amounted to only 6 per cent of total trade. Petroleum from Trinidad and rice from British Guiana are the main items. The economies have all been geared to metropolitan markets and sources of supply. During the days of Federation a customs union plan was drawn up but the breakup of the Federation prevented its implementation.

After this very brief survey of the characteristics and problems of the Caribbean economies, I think it legitimate to draw three conclusions.

First, structural transformation, even in Trinidad and Tobago and Jamaica, has still a long way to go—in spite of the relatively high *per capita* income.

Second, the economies are very dependent, not only structurally in the sense that there is a high ratio of foreign trade to Gross Domestic Product, but also in that there is great reliance on foreign private capital inflows and foreign aid, there is little financial and monetary autonomy, and there are still important gaps in the domestic financial structure. Foreign decision-making is all-pervasive and touches many parts of economic and financial life.

Third, because people have begun to taste the fruits of development as a result of the fortuitous combination of circumstances of the 1950's, any slowing down in the pace of development is fraught with dangers of social and political unrest. The development effort in the years ahead has to be intensified in order to accommodate the rising population with their heightened expectations of material improvement; in order to compensate for the expected decline in the rate of growth of the leading mineral export sectors of bauxite and petroleum; in order to compensate for the removal of opportunities for emigration; and in order to preserve the intrinsically valuable institutions of political democracy and a free trade-union movement.

In order to summarize the foregoing and to promote clarity

of thought, let us now recall the principal structural and institutional characteristics and the major problems of the Caribbean economies relevant to economic planning. Let us further very schematically divide these into three types: those typical of many underdeveloped countries, those typical of small open economies, and those peculiar to the Caribbean. As in all classifications, the distinction between the three types of characteristics is somewhat rough. For example, a developed country may have one or more of the characteristics listed under all three heads, while a large underdeveloped country may exhibit some of the characteristics of small open economies, and so on. The purpose of the classification is purely that of convenience.

1. Typical of many underdeveloped countries:
   (a) an unfavourable ratio between population on the one hand and the stock of capital and of natural resources on the other hand (the Malthusian constraint);
   (b) the dualism of the economic structure as reflected in the varying levels of productivity in different sectors and in the large volume of unemployed, whose productivity is of course zero;
   (c) a domestic agricultural sector, the growth of whose production is lagging behind the increase in demand for food;
   (d) the absence of a developed capital market.

2. Typical of small open economies:
   (a) a high ratio of foreign trade to Gross Domestic Product;
   (b) the domination of the export trade and in some cases the whole economy by one particular export—petroleum in Trinidad and Tobago, bauxite in Jamaica, sugar in Barbados and the Leewards, bananas in the Windwards;
   (c) the absence of a diversified resource base and the narrowness of domestic markets;
   (d) the almost complete lack of domestic interindustry transactions, most transactions being with the outside world;
   (e) the possibility of the export of savings as a result of the branch nature of banking and financial institutions, the automatic functioning of the currency system, and the absence of rigid exchange controls;

(*f*) as a corollary of (*e*), the absence of serious domestically generated inflationary pressures.

3. Peculiar to the West Indies:

   (*a*) the dichotomy between plantation and peasant agriculture, a peculiarly West Indian manifestation of dualism;

   (*b*) a high-cost export agriculture, sheltered by special and other preferential arrangements in the U.K. and Canadian markets;

   (*c*) the firm commitment by present leaders to full-blown political democracy and a free trade-union movement;

   (*d*) the pressure to generalize wage rates 'obtaining in the modern sector, but which are beyond the capacity of the less advanced sectors to pay;

   (*e*) the sharply rising expectations of the population as a result of long contact with and proximity to the Western way of life;

   (*f*) the dependence on foreign capital for the development of the mineral-producing, manufacturing and, to some extent, the sugar industries and the consequent large gap between the domestic product and the national income;

   (*g*) the nature of the public finance system as a consequence of large educational and other recurrent expenditures, revenue foregone through tax incentives and the diseconomies of scale in providing administrative services for small populations.

Having set out the characteristics of the economies very baldly, we may now summarize the problems of the Caribbean in equally bald fashion:

1. The Caribbean economies, in spite of their relatively high *per capita* income, still need to undergo further transformation, especially in view of the slowing down in the rate of growth of the leading mineral-exporting sectors and the disappearance of opportunities for emigration.

2. However broadly or narrowly defined, the Caribbean illustrates many of the characteristics of small open economies as well as some of those of the large underdeveloped countries, and has many peculiar features of its own as well.

3. These peculiarities include the obsessive urge for North American standards of consumption; the dichotomy between plantation and peasant agriculture; the dependence of export agriculture on Commonwealth Preference and special marketing arrangements; the influence exercised by the wage levels in the dominant enclave sectors on the rest of the economy; the peculiar nature of the public finance system; and the great dependence on foreign capital.

In the following chapter, I propose to show how these various characteristics and problems affect the approach to economic planning in the area.

CHAPTER IV: PROBLEMS OF ECONOMIC PLANNING IN THE CARIBBEAN

THIS last chapter discusses some of the implications for economic planning and economic policy raised by the characteristics of the Caribbean economies, in particular their small size and their external dependence. I hope that some of what I have to say will be of general applicability to the problems and opportunities in other small open economies.

First of all, I shall discuss the rationale, objectives, and limitations of planning in small open economies and go on to discuss the techniques of planning appropriate to such countries. Third, I shall outline what I consider to be the appropriate strategy of development in the Caribbean. Fourth, I shall briefly assess the two examples of overall planning in the Caribbean. And I shall end by discussing the problems involved in implementing the plans.

Rationale Objectives and Limitations of Planning in Small Open Economies

Jamaica and Trinidad and Tobago have recently formulated comprehensive Five-Year Plans covering both the public and private sectors. Both plans are now in their first year of implementation. The other territories have public sector development programmes. More recently an attempt has been made to estimate the ten-year capital requirements of the Eastern Caribbean.[1]

In the remainder of this chapter I propose to discuss the kind of overall planning that has taken place in Trinidad and Jamaica and which will at some time take place in British

[1] O'Loughlin, *A Survey of Economic Potential and Capital Needs.*

Guiana and possibly Barbados. The other economies are so tiny and so simple that only public sector programmes are necessary.

No one will deny the necessity for governments drawing up multi-annual capital expenditure programmes. This is done even at the level of local authorities in the U.K. and North America. The rationale of a time perspective longer than one year lies in the fact that the time span between inception and final completion of many capital works may run into several years.

Moreover, capital expenditures in the public sector usually give rise to recurrent expenditures for their operation and maintenance subsequent to completion. Hence even in public sector programmes it is important to look ahead and forecast likely trends in recurrent revenue and expenditure. These financial forecasts may well involve national income forecasting, so that even public sector planning may shade over into overall planning.

While public sector planning may be generally acceptable, the wider kind of overall planning has not usually commanded the same degree of assent. I shall therefore attempt very briefly to give the rationale as well as the limitations of overall planning in small open economies such as those of the larger Caribbean territories.

I shall define planning as the formulation and execution of a consistent set of interrelated measures designed to achieve certain specific economic and social goals. If planning is defined in this way, its most important goal in any underdeveloped country is to achieve as rapidly as possible transformation of the economy, and the possibility of such transformation in turn requires structural and institutional change. Structural changes, as we have indicated above, mean major shifts in the composition of output, the distribution of the labour force, the composition of exports and imports; the forging of linkages between economic sectors; the raising of productivity in lagging sectors and regions; increasing the savings ratio; and above all, changing the direction of investment. Institutional changes are required to create new types of markets, new incentives, new skills, new instruments for mobilizing resources, new attitudes, and increased mobility and responsiveness of factors of production to price and income opportunities. Such institutions include land tenure, marketing, co-operatives, technical schools, and new financial and administrative instruments, to mention only a few.

The market mechanism, working unaided, will, by the very definition of underdevelopment, be unable to generate structural and institutional changes at the pace required by development. On these grounds alone, planning, if it is to mean anything, must encompass the whole economy and take account of, and attempt to influence, decisions in the private as well as the public sector.

In terms of the economic variables involved, structural change is likely to be facilitated by projections of the national output and its most important component sectors and of changes in the distribution of expenditure on the national product. The projection gives us a picture of the structure of the economy as we would like to see it at the end of the plan period. Such projections are an essential part of overall planning. Since economic relationships are very complicated, the projections must obey certain tests of consistency. A consistent set of projections can be of guidance in planning whether they serve as guides to the decision-making processes of the public and private sectors or whether they are in fact targets to be enforced through government fiat. Therefore projections have value independently of the relative importance of the public and private sectors or of the extent to which the government influences, controls, or even coerces the decisions of private producers. Even when projections are not being used as targets, they are important in illuminating the consequences of alternative policies. They give indications of the amount of investment and thus of the volume of domestic and foreign savings required to achieve any specified programme. By the same token they set limits on the practicable size of a programme by indicating the needed amounts of foreign private capital and foreign aid. They can indicate bottlenecks within the economy which are liable to check general economic progress, such as domestic food production, or the impossibility of increasing exports by more than a certain given amount. They can assist in making very rough forecasts of the volume of employment likely to be yielded by a programme through adjusting changes in output by sector by expected changes in productivity. They can be of help in predicting government revenues since different sectors make different contributions to the Exchequer. And, finally, they can have a powerful energizing value on the private sector by revealing to them what increases in production and investment it is possible to achieve, given certain assumptions.

An integrated and consistent set of projections therefore helps overall planning and decision-making by both the public and the private sectors by showing what is feasible. But this is by no means all. National planning involves principally two more things. First, it must be an efficient plan in that, given the objectives, including a certain degree of structural change of the economy, it must allocate resources so as to maximize the return or minimize the cost. The difficulty of efficient resource allocation again arises from the failure of the market mechanism to reflect true long-run social costs and benefits. A whole set of investment criteria has been put forward in recent years incorporating such corrections. But the application of such criteria is hampered both by their logical inadequacy and by the difficulty of applying them statistically. And Chenery has shown that a really efficient plan requires the application of complicated 'linear programming' techniques, involving the use of accounting prices which reflect the true social costs of factors of production.[2] While the Chenery approach seems logically sound, I know of no actual national plan which has been formulated along these lines, although in some countries use has been made of accounting prices in planning certain limited sectors of the economy (especially manufacturing) and in formulating investment priorities. One is forced to conclude that it is relatively easy to produce a 'consistent' plan but very difficult to produce an ideally 'efficient' one.

[2] H. B. Chenery, 'Comparative Advantage and Development Policy', *American Economic Review*, March 1961.

Apart from this, however, there is the important aspect of how to *implement* the required structural changes in the economy. Assuming the economy has an important private sector, there are several ways available. First, the public sector, provided it can secure the necessary resources, can implement its own part of the National Plan, for example its investment programme in infrastructure and directly productive activities, its provision of credit and development finance to private individuals in agriculture or industry, its creation of new or adaptation of existing institutions. Moreover, the private sector can benefit from the 'information' provided in the plan and adjust its volume and pattern of savings and investment accordingly. This is what is supposed to take place under 'indicative planning'. But, more often than not, indicative planning has to be supplemented by various sticks and carrots, deterrents and incentives. Such deterrents and incentives can operate through fiscal, monetary, tariff, and foreign exchange policies. The last is often the most powerful, since governments in underdeveloped countries tend to be short of foreign exchange and can strongly influence the direction of investment by granting or withholding foreign exchange for particular investment projects.

Planning therefore requires the making of a complicated set of consistent projections of the economy and its component parts, and of devising various measures to influence the private sector to realize the projections.

Those who stress the use of uncorrected market mechanisms and private initiative often argue that programming (i.e. the making of a set of consistent overall and sectoral projections) is unnecessary. All that is required, so this argument runs, is limited institutional change designed to increase incentives and maximize the rate of investment, combined with monetary and fiscal policy ensuring every year an *ex-ante* balance between desired saving and desired investment to prevent inflation and balance of payments difficulties.

This view of the nature of economic policy is too limited in that it attaches importance only to the most aggregative kind of balance, that between total demand and total supply. This

123

approach may be adequate in a developed country but would in the majority of cases be incapable of achieving rapid economic and structural transformation of a society. In this kind of situation other balances become important, e.g. the balance between the demand for and the supply of labour (the employment balance) or for that matter sectoral balances such as the demand for and supply of building materials and machinery in the investment component of final demand, the demand for and supply of specific commodities in the consumption component of final demand, and the various demands and supplies of intermediate products. In addition, even within the global balances of savings and investment, exports and imports, the labour force and the supply of jobs, there are certain specific balances. For example, it is not enough to know that exports and imports will balance: it may also be necessary to know whether certain *specific* imported inputs will be available. Again *aggregate* savings and aggregate investment may be in balance *ex-ante* but the capital market will be impotent to bring savings and investment together where savings are highly specific to certain production sectors. Finally, even if there is enough unemployed labour to fill all the available new job opportunities, the absence of certain highly specific skills may frustrate the entire development programme.

The sceptic may grant this as a general proposition. But he may go on to ask the following question: 'In small open economies with automatic currency systems where, in consequence, the rate of growth of G.D.P. is tied to the rate of growth of exports, and where the money supply depends on the state of the balance of payments, is it not enough that aggregate savings should be in balance with aggregate investment at a high level?' The external balance, the sceptic will go on to say, and the sectoral balances in respect of intermediate goods, investment and consumption will take care of themselves. Almost by definition the external balance will not present problems since, the money supply being governed by the state of the balance of payments, there can be no *ex-ante* excess of domestic expenditure over total available resources, since the rate of growth of G.D.P. is tied to that of exports. Nor can there be any bottlenecks in respect of specific intermediate goods because these can be easily imported.

These considerations have real force and rest upon a very important insight into the problems of planning. For, in any economy which is impelled by lagging export demand to industrialize on the basis of import-substitution, bottlenecks in respect of imported final and intermediate goods are bound to arise, giving rise to all sorts of structural difficulties. This has been an important element in the arguments of the structuralist school of thought on inflation in Latin America. Where the desired rate of growth is faster than that permitted by the balance of payments, there is a very strong case for sectoral programming and use of selective policies because reliance on aggregate instruments of monetary and fiscal policy is inconsistent with efforts to achieve that faster desired growth rate.

Planning in this type of economy must rest on a firm and detailed knowledge of interindustry transactions and the input-output table becomes an absolute necessity. Here, too, planning requires more detailed governmental intervention than in the open economy, in order to identify bottlenecks, stimulate lagging sectors and allocate scarce resources according to priorities.

While in a small open economy with an automatic currency system there will always be balance in external payments, other sectoral imbalances will certainly arise. The most obvious is that between the demand for and the supply of labour. The existence of this imbalance should be quite obvious in an economy suffering from structural unemployment, whatever may be its size and whatever may be the character of its monetary and fiscal policies. Second, and even more important, there will be specific shortages of skilled and professional labour, so that even an overall approach to the demand-supply balance in the labour market would be misleading. Third, it is always useful to have a good idea of likely demands for intermediate services, especially public utilities such as electricity and transport. For even in open economies bottlenecks can occur in respect of the supply of goods and services which are not easily importable.

An integrated set of overall and sectoral projections is therefore desirable in planning in all underdeveloped countries, including very small open economies. For as we have seen, projections are important in revealing *implications* of alternative courses of action and of alternative policies. Thus to know that an x per cent increase in manufacturing production entails a y per cent increase in exports of manufactures is an enormously important thing to the policy-maker. Even in an open economy, to know that an x per cent rate of growth in G.D.P. will lead to a deficit of y per cent in the balance of payments indicates the practicable size of the programme, given the amount of aid and capital inflow that can reasonably be expected. Again, as we have seen, a forecast of revenue trends is facilitated by sectoral projections since different sectors differ widely in their contribution to government revenues. In industrial planning too, a knowledge of interindustry relationships is very useful. Projections, even in small open economies, may by providing information help the businessman to capture 'external economies', where for example he learns from a set of projections that x per cent rate of growth in the production of certain consumer goods entails a y per cent increase in the demand for steel. This may highlight the possibility of producing steel on an economic basis since he will know that demand for steel will expand as a result of the programme.

Even if planning may have to be less detailed and a knowledge of interindustry relationships less extensive in a small open economy than in the larger inward-looking ones, planning does not necessarily become simpler. The *making of projections*, as we shall soon see, may be less difficult; but the *implementation* of the plan is more difficult because of a smaller degree of control over the situation. These limitations derive from the relatively large volume of external as compared to domestic transactions and from the lack of control over the monetary and financial systems.

First of all, it is very difficult indeed to predict developments in the external sector, from which the entire economy derives its momentum. And even if what appears to be a realistic forecast is made, there is by definition no way of influencing the behaviour of demand originating in this sector. There is also the difficulty of predicting changes in the commodity terms of trade, especially when such changes take the form of upward movements in import prices.

Second, such an economy may depend to an important extent on inflows of both private foreign capital and foreign aid. The planner can estimate the likely volume of these two magnitudes; but he can do little about influencing the outcome of his predictions.

Third, the monetary system may not be fully autonomous and domestic expenditure may be restricted to the rate of growth of export income by the workings of an automatic mechanism.

The absence of exchange controls and the fact of free convertibility of the currency in unlimited amounts at fixed rates of exchange may lead to an uncontrollable outflow of funds and increase the need for foreign long-term borrowing or aid. There may, however, be compensations in a dependent monetary system arising from the ability of the commercial banks (if they are branches of overseas banks) to finance automatically any excess of domestic expenditure over domestic output by moving funds from head office into the country. But it should be noted that, as in the case of foreign private capital inflow, the decision rests not with the borrowing country but with an outside person or body.

Resource-mobilization will be also made difficult by the absence of a capital market and may make necessary excessive reliance on foreign aid.

And finally, in this context the absence of exchange and trade controls may deprive the planners of one of the most powerful means of influencing the direction of investment.

We may summarize by saying that small open economies just as large closed economies need to plan for structural and institutional change. But in the former case there are greater difficulties in implementing the desired structural changes. Accordingly, more reliance has to be placed on securing the cooperation of the private sector and of large foreign investors than may be necessary in the latter case. Further, more emphasis will have to be placed on the adaptation of the monetary and financial system to ensure a greater degree of control, within the limits set by the need to pursue outward-looking policies.

There are several interesting technical problems raised by programming in a small open economy. I do not have either the time or the inclination to discuss them comprehensively. For, although the programming part of planning is perhaps the most difficult *intellectually*, I believe that the problems of implementation encounter much more serious *practical* difficulties. Moreover, Dudley Seers has dealt adequately with these problems elsewhere. I shall therefore treat this subject very briefly.

The first is the choice of a proper accounting framework for projections. Here there are two extremes. The first is the aggregative national income approach. The second is the input-output table. The first we have seen to be of little value. And the second requires too much information. It is also unnecessary since one of the characteristics of the Caribbean economies (as of most small open economies) is that foreign transactions are much more important than interindustry domestic transactions. An ingenious compromise has been worked out by Dudley Seers,[3] the distinguished U.N. planning economist, who has developed a simplified input-output table where the essential interindustry transactions in each of the major sectors stand out. Moreover projections do not have to be made by inverting the matrix but can be done on a trial by error iterative basis. This gives a great deal of flexibility with respect to the choice of coefficients, thus bringing the use of judgment into exercise.

Second, there is the set of problems relating to whether projections should be in current prices or constant prices. These problems are quite fundamental but would take too long to discuss. I would, however, like to emphasize that a projection in current prices requires the making of assumptions both

[3] See his 'Economic Programming in a Newly Independent Country', *Social and Economic Studies*, March 1962, and his forthcoming paper on 'An Accounting System for Projections in a Specialized Exporter of Primary Products'.

about changes in export and import prices and about the relationships between wage rates, employment, prices, and productivity sector by sector. And this in turn presupposes an explicit model of the working of the economy. Hence the importance to planning of developing models of the functioning of the economy which can be statistically studied.

The importance of making projections in current prices derives principally from the need to make realistic estimates of the government's budget surplus and of the deficit in the balance of payments, especially the latter.

Third, programming ought to be very flexible in such an economy because of the likelihood of sudden major but unanticipated changes in external demand, the effects of such changes on government revenues and the unpredictability of inflows of external financial resources. This means that the projections ought to be constantly revised, in fact, every year at the same time as the annual budget is being prepared. Such revisions are automatically carried out when the plan is of the type known as a 'rolling plan'—that is, one that is annually carried forward by one year, as in Puerto Rico. The real issue is not whether a 'rolling plan' should be prepared, but whether it should be officially published every year as a new 'plan'. I believe that the annual exercise of revising the projections and carrying them forward by one year should be undertaken within the planning office. It seems to me, however, that a fixed-period plan has much to commend it since, by setting targets and objectives which remain fixed, the planners are probably in a better position to elicit the interest and mobilize the efforts of the private sector and of the population at large who are thereby given clearcut perspectives which do not shift from year to year as under the 'rolling plan'. At the same time, it is clear that, where major deviations from the basic goals of the originally approved plan are imposed by a change in circumstances, official targets should be publicly revised.

Finally, it is almost unnecessary to add that a basic requirement of programming, or indeed of economic policy, in any kind of economy is the availability of a wide range of reliable statistics. Both Jamaica and Trinidad and Tobago are in a much better position in this respect than most other under-developed countries.

So far we have discussed consistent overall projections as a basis for the drawing up of feasible programmes. We have said nothing about the choice of projects or the allocation of resources as between sectors. The problems raised here are the same as in other countries and it is therefore unnecessary to go into detail. A few comments will be in order.

First, project planning in the public sector is just as important as the macro-economic type of planning we have just dealt with. Proper feasibility studies, proper estimating, and rigid control of costs are obviously necessary.

Second, in allocating total revenue to the different kinds of governmental expenditure, a proper balance has to be struck between productive and non-productive expenditures. Further, estimated recurrent expenditures associated with various kinds of capital expenditures must be taken into account. In this connection, education raises rather difficult problems, since current expenditure on this service in fact represents an investment in the only reliable resource of small countries such as the Caribbean—their people.

Third, in a small open economy it is necessary to select industries for special encouragement. This must be done with care and account must be taken of comparative advantage conceived in dynamic terms. This means that account must be taken not only of employment, but also of the utilization of local raw materials and of the extent to which export markets can be found. These last two criteria may often result in the establishment of capital-intensive industries, because the utilization of domestic materials may involve complex processes (for example petrochemicals or aluminium) and because the best prospects for growth in demand are often to be found in technologically dynamic but capital-intensive industries whose products have a high income-elasticity of demand.

In addition it may be necessary, as in Puerto Rico, to plan for the establishment of interdependent industrial complexes. A single industry—for example, oil-refining—may of itself be marginal, or even unprofitable; but if it becomes part of a complex of related industries—such as oil-refining, petro-chemicals, and plastics—it can be successful.

Such industrial planning requires the carrying out of feasibility studies in which economists co-operate with industrial engineers, chemical engineers, accountants, and other specialists. Unlike macro-economic planning, industrial planning cannot be carried out by economists alone, but requires the skills of highly trained engineers

Development Strategy in the Caribbean

A National Plan must be based on some overall strategy of development which sets the framework for more specific objectives and more precise policies. The strategy of development ought to flow from an analysis of the characteristics and problems of an economy and of its recent history. Among the characteristics size is always important, as I have sought to show above.

I shall discuss the strategy which I consider appropriate for the Caribbean over the next decade or so, under the following heads: Policy Decision on Degree of Openness, Manufacturing, Employment, Agriculture, Relations with International Corporations, and Generation of Local Centres of Decision Making, Education and Training, and Output versus Employment.

Policy Decision on Degree of Openness. From what I have said in this and previous chapters it is clear that there is scope for the Caribbean countries to reduce somewhat the degree of openness of their economies. It is true that the small size of the domestic market and the need to rely heavily on exports rule out an insulation of the domestic economy through the imposition of a wide all-embracing network of restrictions on imports and foreign payments. We do, however, have to use the tariff to protect domestic industries and to reduce imports of inessentials and luxuries. Further, acceptance of the fundamental reality of an open economy does not imply acceptance of orthodox financial, commercial, and monetary policies according to the rules of the game laid down by the advanced countries. In other words, there is some scope for varying the degree of openness, policywise. As we saw in the previous chapter, it is necessary to acquire greater monetary autonomy so that the rate of growth of domestic expenditure will cease to be so rigidly tied to the rate of growth of exports. Such a limited application of the disequilibrium system pivoting around a massive housing construction programme seems to be required if employment is to expand sufficiently. The only alternative to such a limited application of the disequilibrium system is to reduce the rate of growth of population.

Manufacturing. I have tried to show that small open economies can achieve transformation only on the basis of developing exports of manufactured goods. For Trinidad and Tobago and Jamaica this has become vital in the face of the slowing down of the rate of growth of mineral production (oil in Trinidad and bauxite in Jamaica), and the limits set to the expansion of the traditional agricultural exports by external marketing considerations. I also indicated the sharp limits to import-substitution set by the lack of a diversified resource base and the absence of opportunities for economies of scale in industrial programmes devoted to the home market alone.

It should be noted in passing that the attitude of well-entrenched commercial interests can also often further restrict the sales on the local market of locally produced manufactures. This happens because each local seller of imported goods wants to be able to offer a different 'brand' of the same product. He also wants to be in a position to offer a wide variety of styles, etc., between which the consumer can choose. This means that even where a local manufacturer operating under fairly high tariff protection may be able to offer a product comparable in quality and price to the imported goods, the local distributor is prepared to continue importing. This aggravates the inherent difficulties of import-substitution in a small country. The local commercial interests can effectively block the sales of an efficient local producer. Under these circumstances a judicious application of quantitative restrictions may be the only means of providing an assured market outlet for the locally produced goods.

Let me not be misunderstood, however. To say that the development of manufacturing exports should be the objective of policy is not to overlook further possibilities of import-substitution in respect of domestic agriculture, food-processing, and manufacturing. All that I am saying is that the feasible limit of import-substitution is likely to be reached before the economies have undergone a high degree of transformation and before all the surplus labour is absorbed, given the foreseeable rate of growth of mineral exports. And, clearly, it is important to start developing manufactured exports as early as possible. Indeed a given increment of export-creation now is more valuable than the same increment of import-substitution —although the two things may have identical effects on income,[4] the balance of payments, and on employment—for the important reason that, exporting manufactures being more difficult than producing them for the home market, the earlier the learning process starts the better. This implies that an appropriate strategy has to give emphasis to the building up of institutions for the promotion and financing of exports of manufactures.

Employment. Exporting manufactures raises the question of employment. If manufactured exports are to be developed, they must be produced cheaply at the lowest *money* cost of production, which of course may not always coincide with the lowest *social* cost. Given the existing wage levels in Jamaica and Trinidad and given the fact that modern technology, which is capital-intensive, yields production at the lowest money cost of production, it appears that capital-intensive methods will often be inescapable. This means that, even if manufactured exports expand very rapidly, they could still not expand fast enough to cope with the unemployment problem, at least for the next decade or so. It is therefore necessary to take special measures to deal with the unemployment problem. Construction, which is highly labour-intensive, suggests itself; and it is therefore necessary to give special emphasis to house construction and to public works programmes as a means of absorbing the labour surplus. House construction has important backward-linkage

[4] To the extent that enterprises producing manufactures for export are foreign-owned, we should of course allow for the leakage abroad of foreign profits.

133

effects through its effect in stimulating the demand for the output of the building-materials industries and for fittings, furnishings, etc. Moreover, a large part of the total construction expenditure is on local factors of production and on locally produced building materials.

Agriculture. The existence of surplus labour also has to condition the type of development envisaged for the domestic agricultural sector. I have already referred to the dichotomy between plantation and peasant agriculture. While in most islands both plantations and peasants produce export crops, it is the peasant who is primarily responsible for producing food for domestic consumption. But whatever the type of crop produced, there is a vast gulf between plantation and peasant agriculture in terms of capital used per head, technology employed, and therefore yields per man and per acre. The shortcomings of the small farmer as an economic agent are numerous and not peculiar to the West Indies. To a large extent the problem in the West Indies is sociological and can be traced back to the system of slavery and indenture. The peculiar economic and social history of the area has produced a contempt for agriculture among many people and, where it has not done so, it has militated against peasant farming being regarded as a full-time skilled occupation.

In the light of such considerations it has often been suggested that West Indian governments should cease trying to make the small farmer (with five acres or so) efficient and attempt to create twenty-acre or even fifty-acre holdings where the farmer would be intelligent, well-educated, would employ tractors and other equipment, and would use advanced agricultural methods. A viable domestic agriculture, it has been argued, is possible only on the basis of such 'agro-businesses'.

There is much force in this contention and many of the arguments adduced are very persuasive. And in fact there may even be some room for experimentation along these lines. But a general approach on this basis completely overlooks the problem of surplus labour. Such an approach would be feasible only if either manufacturing production could expand fast enough or if manufacturing production were less capital-intensive than it is and has to be. In either alternative there would be room for surplus labour displaced in manufacturing. But, as we have seen, this is not the case.

Moreover, this approach overlooks the vitally important distinction between returns per man and returns per acre. It is elementary that yields per *man* can increase (through, say, a larger holding per man or through the use of machinery) without any increase in yields per *acre*; whereas under most circumstances an increase in yield per acre almost always entails an increase in yields per man, even though the farmer may have to work harder and possibly for longer hours because more intensive cultivation may be required to make the land yield more.

Here we have to invoke the neo-classical theory of factor-proportions, which enjoins us to maximize the yield of the relatively scarce factor, in this case land. In this case the neo-classical argument for the best use of scarce resources happens to coincide with the very practical consideration of employment.

On the other hand, the neo-classical argument on factor-proportions does not help us when we are dealing with the manufacturing sector. This is so for two reasons. First, in the modern sector, wages are out of line with relative factor supplies (a clear violation of a basic neo-classical assumption), whereas in domestic peasant agriculture there is for the most part no wage labour and therefore no possibility of the return to the farmer exceeding his marginal productivity. And, in the second place, it is broadly true that the lowest money costs of production in many manufacturing industries are yielded by capital-intensive methods embodied in technologies which use fixed technical coefficients.

What is really being suggested here is that in very small economies with surplus labour, the strategy of development does not call for an attempt to eliminate dualism from the economic structure over the next decade or so—in the sense of aiming at equalizing output per man as between the advanced and traditional sectors of the economy, but rather for a controlled and conscious dualism envisaging the maintenance of a

135

gap between output per man in the export sector and in the domestic sectors such as domestic agriculture, construction, and public works. In doing this, of course dualism will be mitigated both through the encouragement of higher yields per acre, and so per man, in domestic agriculture and through the creation of employment opportunities in construction: for it must be borne in mind that the existence of a large pool of structurally unemployed labour constitutes the most extreme form of dualism.

The compromise with the modernization process in respect of agriculture and construction which is being advocated here can be contrasted with the approach to agriculture in Puerto Rico where in the last few years there have been tremendous gains in output per man. Agricultural productivity increased at some 6 per cent per annum as a result of the larger size of holding and the introduction of machinery. The situation in Puerto Rico is, however, essentially different from that existing in the British Caribbean. Puerto Rican manufacturing exports can expand at a faster rate, thanks to the free availability of the U.S. market, and Puerto Ricans can migrate freely to the U.S.A. On the other hand, the British islands have much more difficulty in getting export markets and, besides, there is nowhere to go to.

What makes the employment problem so intractable in the Caribbean is that as soon as new jobs are created in the high-wage, high-productivity modern sector, the demand for such jobs increases. In fact, as jobs expand in the cities, there is an increase in the number of unemployed as migrants move in from rural areas and people in low-paid urban jobs demand better-paid jobs.[5] Therefore the development strategy must seek to prevent the drift from rural to urban areas. While many hold that this drift cannot be stopped since it does not derive from an absence of employment opportunities in the rural areas, I believe that migration out of rural areas can be slowed down by making the countryside a better place in which to live. This implies measures to raise output per acre, as well as

[5] Cf. W. A. Lewis, 'Employment Policy in an Under-Developed Area' *Social and Economic Studies*, September, 1958.

the provision of better public amenities and the development of community life.

Relations with International Corporations. An appropriate development strategy would also have to include machinery designed to ensure that the decisions of the large international corporations operating in the area are harmonized with the national interest, not through nationalization or expropriation, but through close consultation with a well-informed government.

The counterpart to the domination of the economy by large international corporations is the small number of local relatively to foreign centres of decision-making. The West Indian economies are dependent not only in the sense that they have a high ratio of foreign trade to Gross Domestic Product, but also in that a large part of the capital stock is owned by foreigners and that financial institutions such as commercial banks and insurance companies are also, for the most part, foreign-owned. If one starts from the value judgment that, apart from the growth of *per capita* income and total employment, it is desirable to generate as many local centres of decision-making as possible in the economic life of the community, it follows that an increase in the share of total investment financed by national savings should be an important objective of policy.

Generation of Local Centres of Decision-Making. To the extent that one accepts these basic premises, a strategy of development for the Caribbean must of necessity emphasize an increase in the proportion of investment derived from national sources of saving. And it must also emphasize the encouragement of local entrepreneurs, the development of locally owned financial institutions, and greater management of the monetary and financial system by the authorities. All of these objectives, it should be noted, can be achieved without necessarily lessening the inflow of foreign capital or affecting the position of existing foreign firms or institutions. The price to be paid for such a generation of a greater number of local centres of decision-making is a greater local savings and entrepreneurial effort, stimulated by governmental measures.

It should be noted, however, that to some extent increased

scope for local decision-making can be achieved without necessarily increasing the proportion of total investment financed from national savings. This could happen, for example, as a result of the growth of joint-venture undertakings, in which local capital, either private or governmental, would participate along with foreign capital.

Education and Training. Next, the development strategy must include the closest possible attention to education and training at all levels. This need is not of course peculiar to the West Indies. We are now inundated with studies from the U.S.A. which purport to show that the high rate of growth of output per man over the last eighty years or so was due not primarily to capital accumulation or even to technical progress but to education. This is not the place to assess the validity of this conclusion or to distinguish between the economic value of scholastic, technical, or on-the-job training. All I want to do here is to emphasize the important role of education and training in the Caribbean where the only resource—apart from oil and bauxite—is the people. It is necessary, however, to point out that emphasis on educational programmes has important consequences for the government's budget, since such programmes entail very high recurrent expenditures.

Output versus Employment. I shall end this discussion of strategy by referring to a question often asked of development planners in the Caribbean—should the goal of a development plan be to raise incomes per head or to increase employment? In a small over-populated economy export prices are determined by the world market and hence the production techniques which yield the lowest money costs of production have to be used. As we have seen, this necessity imposes sharp constraints on the factor-mix in manufacturing industry and may dictate the use of highly capital-intensive techniques which raise output per man but do little to provide direct employment for labour. On the other hand, it would be possible for a large closed economy to give more emphasis to employment creation in the modern sectors by insulating the economy from foreign competition, since in such an economy it would be possible to achieve economies of scale in production for the domestic market where, in any event, the achievement of competitive prices is less important than in the export market.

Moreover there are revenue considerations. Other things being equal, a high rate of growth makes for buoyant government revenues which can be used to provide employment on labour-intensive construction projects. In this connection it seems important to stress that the use of accounting prices (which reflect the true opportunity-cost of labour) for valuing the cost of such projects will certainly involve either direct or indirect subsidies from the Exchequer in order to compensate for the difference between market wage rates and the 'true' price of labour.

We must therefore conclude that under Caribbean conditions a high rate of growth of output, so far from being inimical to, is to a large extent a condition of the maintenance of high levels of employment.

There are of course other important aspects of development strategy in the Caribbean. But I have confined myself to those that flow from what I consider to be the unique characteristics of the West Indian economy, especially its small absolute size.

These are, of course, broad, and perhaps excessively broad, generalizations. But the defect of all analytic formulations of policy choices is that they are too general. The policy-maker has to be acutely aware of the complexity of concrete situations and has to know all the exceptions and all the modifications to the general principles. On the other hand, the virtue of analytic formulations is that they help the policy-maker to see the wood from the trees and thereby help him steer his way through the myriad complexities of the real world.

For my part, I am very much aware of the numerous exceptions to the rules of thumb which I have been trying to develop. For one thing, I consider that there may be room for experimentation with the larger farm unit. There is, I think, also room for experimentation with the handicraft type of manufacturing, although severe organizational difficulties will be encountered in ensuring an even flow of inputs to the producer and an even flow of outputs to the consumer. There is certainly room for more multi-shift working in the larger factories in order to reduce the amount of capital required per man. There may also be room for the small 'backyard' type of industry. There is certainly room for the highly mechanized type of public works construction in situations where the money costs and the time involved in using highly labour-intensive methods in major construction projects would both be exorbitant. But I believe that the main guide-lines which I have outlined should form the basis of the strategy of development appropriate to at least the two largest territories of Jamaica and Trinidad and Tobago.

Review of National Plans of Jamaica and Trinidad and Tobago

It is not my intention to summarize the plans of the West Indies. The documents embodying the plans are all readily available and in any event space would not permit an accurate summary. Instead, I propose to draw attention to some aspects of the new Five-Year Plans of Jamaica and Trinidad and Tobago, the two countries with overall plans using programming techniques.

Let us start with the similarities. First, both plans make use of Dudley Seers' accounting framework for making projections. Second, both plans anticipate a slowing-down in the rate of growth of G.D.P. as compared with the 1950's. In both cases growth rates of G.D.P. of 5 per cent per annum are projected. Third, in both cases, the slowing down in the rate of growth of G.D.P. is the result of the anticipated slowing down in the rate of growth of the mineral export sectors to 3 per cent per annum —bauxite in Jamaica and petroleum in Trinidad. Fourth, in both cases the development of manufacturing exports and the limits to further import substitution are stressed. Fifth, in both cases, the expansion of export agriculture is constrained by the difficulties of increasing sales abroad rather than an inability to increase output. Sixth, both plans envisage a stepping-up of the rate of growth of hitherto stagnant domestic agriculture to 4 per cent or 5 per cent per annum, with the small farmer playing an important role in this sector. Seventh, both plans aim at programmes of rural community development designed to arrest the drift from country to town. Finally, both plans assume that large amounts of government-to-government soft loans will be forthcoming to finance public sector expenditures.

Let us now take the points of difference. First, the Trinidad and Tobago plan makes specific forecasts of employment and envisages that the increase in the labour force over the plan period will be just barely absorbed—with luck. The Jamaica plan makes no employment forecasts, perhaps wisely. Second, the Jamaica plan places more emphasis on the social services, reflecting the greater backlog in respect of primary education and perhaps a stronger consciousness of the need to ward off social discontent. Third, the Jamaica plan proposes a more radical approach to agriculture by bringing pressure to bear on the large estate owner to cultivate his land intensively. Finally, the Jamaica plan envisages a large increase in public sector spending to provide compensation for the loss of migration outlets.

My general view is that, while the two plans are surprisingly similar in objectives and even financing, the Trinidad and Tobago plan is a more educative document in that it discusses more explicitly the various fiscal, monetary, and commercial policies to be pursued and the nature of and limitations to planning in the Caribbean. This plan also spells out very sharply the implications of a diminishing rate of growth of mineral exports and it emphasizes the importance of developing exports of manufactured goods. On the other hand, the Jamaica planners seem much more aware of the social objectives of planning.

Implementation of Plans

I propose to discuss in this final section the implementations of overall plans of the Jamaica and Trinidad and Tobago type. I shall deal first of all with the four fundamental limitations to planning in the Caribbean, then I shall discuss briefly some of the other problems of implementation under the following heads: Administration, Wages Policy, Resource Mobilization, and the Development of Caribbean Economic Co-operation.

The four fundamental limitations to overall planning in the Caribbean are the openness of the economy, the relatively small role played by the public sector, the dependence on foreign commercial capital, and the dominance of international corporations in resource-exploitation—oil in Trinidad and bauxite in Jamaica.

The openness of the economy has several implications for the implementation of development plans. First of all, it means that the projections of external demand can go very far wrong because demand conditions for the country's exports abroad are subject to sudden change. Thus, there may be a major recession in one or more of the major markets of the country or shifts abroad in commercial policy or in the competitive position of the country *vis-à-vis* other suppliers. On the whole, fairly conservative forecasts have to be made after detailed study of demand and supply conditions for each main export commodity. The difficulty of predicting foreign sales is to my mind the most critical limitation of planning in the Caribbean. At the same time, however, because of the fact of foreign ownership of enterprises producing exports, movements in the national income (the income accruing to residents) are less sharp than movements in G.D.P.

Another consequence of the openness of the economy is the possibility of an upward rise in import prices of capital or consumer goods relatively to export prices, with effects on the real value of investment and the real wage level.

In the specific case of the two countries we are discussing, export demand depends overwhelmingly on the prospects for oil, bauxite, and sugar. Fortunately, the market for sugar is fairly well guaranteed at prices designed to cover costs of production of reasonably efficient producers, while the prices of both oil and bauxite are more stable than those of most other primary products.[6] The terms-of-trade effect, operating through a rise in import prices, is however more difficult to predict.

Next, the public sector does not play a very important role in capital formation in either Jamaica or Trinidad. In recent

---

[6] Dudley Seers has pointed out to me that an additional characteristic of the Caribbean is that export income is comparatively stable—in terms of both price and volume—from year to year.

years the shares of the public sector in total capital formation were 10 per cent and 20 per cent respectively. In many other underdeveloped countries, the public sector accounts for as much as 50 per cent or more of total capital formation. The small share of the public sector in the two countries is in part due to the statistical mirage created by the dominance of heavy capital-using mineral sectors such as bauxite and oil in the context of an absolutely small economy. But it is also due to the belief that the public sector should for the most part confine itself to the provision of economic and social overheads, leaving the bulk of directly productive investment to the private sector. As we have already seen, there are important means of influencing the decisions of the private sector so that its actions would be in conformity with the objectives of the plan. Such means generally take the form of the provision of incentives. But what in most other countries is the most powerful tool for directing the private sector—viz. licences to import and to invest—is not available. Planning for the private sector has to be a highly permissive business and the projections have an indicative rather than an imperative nature.

The dependence on inflows of private commercial capital also raises serious problems of implementing the projections. A wide array of tax incentives designed to attract both local and foreign investment in manufacturing and tourism is offered by both countries. And, apart from tax incentives, the foreign investor looks for a well-developed framework of social and economic overheads and basic continuity in government policies and regulations. These conditions are present in both countries.

The problems raised by the dominant role played by the large international corporations producing oil, bauxite, and sugar come under all three of the above heads. Most of the product of these companies is exported and depends upon the vagaries of demand in the world market generally or in particular markets, all the capital is foreign and, of course, the corporations are not part of the public sector. Under these circumstances, the formulation and the implementation of overall development plans depend on the development of

143

effective relationships between the governments and the large international companies. And the development of such relationships depends in turn on the governments acquiring extensive knowledge about the technical conditions under which the companies operate both locally and abroad, and on world supply and demand relationships. Armed with this extensive knowledge, the governments would be in a position to evaluate independently such things as the adequacy of the companies' contribution to government's revenues, their production rates, their employment practices, etc. In large part the rate of production of minerals must be a matter for joint discussion between the government and the companies. A difference of 1 per cent in the annual rate of growth of production of petroleum in Trinidad can make a great deal of difference to the rate of growth of G.D.P., to fiscal revenues, to the balance of payments, etc. For planning to be fully effective, the production plans of the large corporations must become mutually agreed targets rather than mere projections.

Taking all these factors into account, we are forced to conclude that the implementation of plans for the private sector is not as easy in the Caribbean as in other countries.

At the same time however, projections, even *qua* projections, can have a powerful value in guiding business decisions. Through the publication of a national plan the private sector can be made to visualize hitherto unsuspected investment opportunities and the plan can have a powerful educational value and lead to a change in the traditional investment pattern by modifying the attitudes of the private sector.

A National Plan affects not only businessmen. It also affects small farmers, trade unionists, and of course the individual citizen, who may have to dip into his pocket to help finance the plan. It is therefore important in a democratic society to seek a wide basis of general consensus on the objectives and instruments of the plan. This requires a programme of adult education as well as the development of appropriate machinery. Trinidad and Tobago has developed machinery with this end in view. First, a National Economic Advisory Council has been created so that the private sector can advise the government on all matters of national development. Second, the Draft Plan was published for public comment and a forum was called by the government to discuss the comments of the public.

I shall not discuss extensively problems of planning organization or administration, except to draw attention to three things. First, there is an acute shortage, not only of engineers and middle-level personnel, but also of agricultural extension officers. The shortage of extension officers could be one of the biggest obstacles to the fulfilment of a plan relying so heavily on increased production and productivity in the domestic agricultural sector. Second, as in all developing countries, effective planning and co-ordination of economic policy require the utmost clarification of the respective roles of the planning agency, finance ministry, and the other executive ministries and agencies. Third, the public service has been reared in the colonial tradition of avoiding mistakes, performing routine operations, and not taking important and quick decisions. Quite obviously, a new approach by the public service is required in the content of an independent society aiming at rapid economic development. The new approach would have to stress qualities such as initiative, imagination, and speed of decision-making.

The wage issue will also present problems in the implementation of the plan. No country that I know of—except perhaps Sweden and Holland—has been able to implement an effective wages policy.[7] In advanced countries a wages policy is desired primarily as a means of checking inflation. As we have seen, in the Caribbean a rapid rise in wages can check the expansion of employment, can hinder capital formation, and can unbalance the government's budget. A wages policy would be very difficult to implement; but, analytically, the problem resolves itself into one of keeping down wages in the modern sector and using the increase in wages foregone for investment in either the public or the private sector. Economic planning in the Carib-

---

[7] I refer, of course, to pluralistic societies where associations such as trade unions and employers' associations are independent of the state. I understand that the Dutch plan broke down recently.

bean can never be fully effective until such a time as a solution is found for this problem.

The next set of problems is that relating to resource-mobilization. I shall consider the difficulty of the government securing a large enough surplus of recurrent revenue over recurrent expenditure, the absence of a capital market, the phenomenon of 'excess borrowing', and the problem of economic aid. We have already mentioned these problems; but it is necessary to say a few more words about them.

Leaving aside the problems of the smaller grant-in-aid countries, many West Indian governments face difficulties in securing a large enough surplus of recurrent revenue over recurrent expenditure, in spite of the progressive and relatively efficient nature of the fiscal system. This is so, first of all, because the granting of tax incentives to the growing sectors—viz. oil, manufacturing, and tourism—means that, so long as the economy keeps growing, there will be a lag of recurrent revenue behind the growth of G.D.P. The result is that a disproportionate part of the burden of taxation has to fall on personal incomes and personal consumption as against business income. Second, the very implementation of past development programmes, especially in education, has left a heavy burden of recurrent expenditure. And there are always the diseconomies of scale involved in providing administrative services for small territories.

Next, there is no capital market and this makes it difficult to raise capital funds for both the public and private sectors. Moreover, there would always be difficulties in developing a capital market in a very small country, since the volume of domestic transactions would be small and since the market is hardly likely to have sufficient breadth.

Further, the openness of the financial system, including currency boards, central banks which behave like currency boards, the branch type of commercial banks, insurance companies which invest a large part of their income abroad—all this, combined with the absence of rigid exchange controls, makes for an outflow of local savings while the countries have to borrow money from abroad. This constitutes the phenomenon of 'excess borrowing'. The borrowing abroad does not lead to any net transfer of real resources in that the long-term liabilities are matched by an increase in foreign exchange reserves or the accumulation of other foreign assets. This is quite obviously an uneconomic procedure, since the rate of interest on the long-term loans is likely to exceed the income from the short-term assets. While excess borrowing is connected with the under-developed state of the capital market, it springs fundamentally from the absence of effective exchange controls.

Finally, under the head of resource mobilization, there is the large financial gap to be filled by foreign aid. This gap is the counterpart of the difficulty of generating sufficient public savings and the difficulty of utilizing all domestic private savings for domestic investment. In both the Trinidad and Tobago and the Jamaica plans the financial gap in the public sector programme is larger than the direct foreign exchange component of public sector projects. This is not surprising, for seldom is the need for foreign exchange measured by the direct foreign exchange component of public sector development programmes.

The difficulties of mobilizing resources seem to point to the desirability of establishing a national insurance fund (excluding unemployment benefits in order to prevent bankruptcy) under which contributions would exceed benefits so that a fund for capital formation can be built up. This is one of the most important objectives of the new scheme proposed by the Province of Quebec and adopted by the Federal Parliament for application to the whole of Canada.

I shall end by reverting to a theme stressed in an earlier chapter. As small countries attempting to industrialize on the basis of export creation, the West Indian economies should have every incentive to engage in regional forms of industrial planning. Whether such co-operation takes the forms of a customs union, free trade area, or limited preferential area does not matter too much initially.[8]

[8] Dudley Seers has pointed out to me that, even if Caribbean co-operation is pursued, this should not preclude seeking out trade agree-

In the second chapter I dealt quite generally with the economics of integration between underdeveloped countries and tried to indicate the likely sources of benefits. I therefore shall not attempt to go over the ground again, except to state very baldly what seem to me to be the four fundamental issues raised by a movement towards Caribbean integration.

The first and most obvious is the development of adequate efficient and cheap transport links by air and sea within the region. The second would be the devising of measures to safeguard *existing* industries—since, as we have seen, the important thing is to widen the market for *new* industries. The third is the application of measures for dealing with the problem of polarization—assisting the less developed territories—either through the deliberate creation of poles of growth in territories where there is some scope for modern manufacturing industry or through fiscal transfers, or through what McIntyre has termed 'export-substitution'.[9]

This last approach involves mutual agreement between territories to specialize in activities for which they are specially suited. For example, a larger territory with advantages in manufacturing may renounce the right to increase production of an agricultural export also produced by a smaller territory which would in return admit the manufactured exports of the larger territory duty-free into its own market. The final issue is the introduction of a certain degree of co-ordinated industrial and agricultural planning designed to avoid unnecessary duplication. It is simply bad economics for each territory to have its own cement plant, oil refinery, or steel mill.

As a start towards economic co-ordination, some agreement can in the meantime be reached on reducing the self-defeating competition among the territories in respect of the provision of tax-holidays for attracting foreign capital.

I have no doubt that these approaches are worth serious and urgent consideration by the governments concerned, even though, as one who as a civil servant has learnt painfully to be

ments to export manufactures to either individual Latin American countries or to the Latin American free trade area.

[9] See McIntyre, *Decolonization and Trade Policy.*

realistic, I do not underestimate the enormous difficulties involved, particularly in the light of previous abortive attempts to integrate some of the countries politically as well as economically.

I should like to end on another sober note. It cannot be repeated too often that the Caribbean, even if it becomes integrated economically, will still be a region that experiences a great deal of external dependence. Even though in an integrated region a slightly less dependent pattern of development might become possible, yet the reliance on overseas markets will still be great. The world market for manufactured goods, with all its hazards and all its opportunities, will still remain to be conquered. And, even when the region rids itself of dependence on external aid, it may still be an important recipient of private capital inflow.

We may end by summarizing the argument of this last chapter in the following broad propositions:

1. Planning for structural change is just as important in small open economies as in larger less open ones. But there is the paradox that it is simpler to formulate plans but harder to implement them in the former than in the latter.

2. Development strategy in the Caribbean involves the utmost possible promotion of exports of manufactures. But this in itself cannot solve the unemployment problem. Additional requirements for a solution are a slight reduction in the degree of openness, greater emphasis on housing construction, and an awareness of the surplus labour supply in formulating agricultural policies. Dualism cannot be eliminated overnight. It has to be controlled.

3. Implementation of a National Plan in the Caribbean requires close collaboration with the private sector and with international investors.

4. Financial and monetary institutions need to be adapted to ensure greater domestic direction of economic policy and to assist in mobilizing for domestic use domestically generated financial resources.

5. An incomes policy may be necessary to break the link between wage levels in the leading sector and in other sectors

and to secure that what would have been won in wage increases in the leading sector is invested productively within the economy.

6. It is urgently necessary to achieve a greater degree of economic co-operation in the Caribbean—although it should be recognized that such a consummation will not absolve the area from a large measure of external dependence, especially on outside markets for manufactured goods.

Date Due